STUDIES IN ROMANCE LANGUAGES: 30
John E. Keller, *Editor*

BEYOND THE METAFICTIONAL MODE

DIRECTIONS IN THE MODERN SPANISH NOVEL

Robert C. Spires

360439

THE UNIVERSITY PRESS OF KENTUCKY

Copyright © 1984 by The University Press of Kentucky

Scholarly publisher for the Commonwealth,
serving Bellarmine College, Berea College, Centre
College of Kentucky, Eastern Kentucky University,
The Filson Club, Georgetown College, Kentucky
Historical Society, Kentucky State University,
Morehead State University, Murray State University,
Northern Kentucky University, Transylvania University,
University of Kentucky, University of Louisville,
and Western Kentucky University.

Editorial and Sales Offices: Lexington, Kentucky 40506-0024

Library of Congress Cataloging in Publication Data

Spires, Robert C.
    Beyond the metafictional mode.

    Bibliography: p.
    Includes index.
    1. Spanish fiction—20th century—History and criticism. 2. Fiction—Technique. I. Title.
PQ6144.S648 1984   863'.64'09   84-7565
ISBN 0-8131-1520-5

To Jeffrey R. and Leslie Ann

Contents

Preface ix

Introduction: The Metafictional Mode 1

1. Violations and Pseudo-Violations: *Quijote*, *Buscón*, and "La novela en el tranvía" 18

2. Fiction on a Palimpsest: *Niebla* 33

3. Codes versus Modes: *Locura y muerte de nadie* and *La novia del viento* 45

4. Rebellion against Models: *Don Juan* and *Orestes* 58

5. Process as Product: *Juan sin Tierra* 72

6. Reading-into-Being: *La cólera de Aquiles* 89

7. Product Preceding Process: *El cuarto de atrás* 107

Afterwords 125

Notes 129

Bibliography 141

Index 149

Preface

Although my interest in metafiction was inspired by contemporary novels, when I began this study I found I had to establish some kind of historical view before attempting to deal with present-day metafictional works. As others have already pointed out, the term metafiction invaded our critical vocabulary around 1970, yet the textual strategies involved in turning fiction back onto itself can be traced to at least the sixteenth century. The discrepancy between the earlier examples of what we now call metafiction and the recent coining of the term perhaps can be explained by the complementary evolution of textual strategies and reader expectations. That is, the opposition between the first expression of the mode and the expectations of readers was so great that a long process of reception was required. But just as the initial readings were continued and enriched through further receptions from generation to generation, so the strategies fed on one another. The whole process has culminated, from our present perspective, in the current obsession with novelistic self-commentary. This book, then, chronicles such an evolutionary process in the Spanish novel from the beginning of the seventeenth century up to the 1980s; it analyzes the development of the metafictional mode into the recent self-referential Spanish novel.

The sources for my theoretical/critical project are somewhat eclectic, and, although there is probably a predominance of names associated with structuralism and semiotics, they include representatives of poststructuralism and hermeneutics. The references in the text identify who these people are, yet two theorists whose ideas have been fundamental to my own thinking deserve to be singled out here: Gérard Genette and Félix Martínez Bonati. I have included in the bibliography some works not directly quoted but whose imprint may be detected in my commentaries. I should also note that in all likelihood I have failed to recognize the contribution of others merely because their ideas have now become so much a part of me that I have forgotten where I discovered them. I can only hope that any such person will view his or her omission as the compliment it really is.

The purely theoretical section of this book is the Introduction. There I address the question of narrative mode and propose a modal definition of metafiction. This section represents an attempt both to summarize others' ideas and to propose my own admittedly derivative theories.

The chapters following the Introduction feature detailed analyses of from one to three works each, with briefer analyses of novels pertaining to the same general category. The format is chronological, although chronology is not strictly adhered to in the final three chapters devoted to novels published in the 1970s and 1980s. In order of appearance, then, there is one chapter each on the precursors of the twentieth century (the *Quijote, El Buscón,* and "La novela en el tranvía"), on the Generation of '98 *(Niebla),* on the vanguardist period (*Locura y muerte de nadie* and *La novia del viento*), on the postwar period (*Don Juan* and *Un hombre que se parecía a Orestes*), and finally three chapters on the last decade: novels foregrounding the act of writing (*Juan sin Tierra*), the act of reading *(La cólera de Aquiles),* and the act of discourse itself (*El cuarto de atrás*). Although the format is designed to provide a historical view, the examples are selective rather than comprehensive. Generally I have chosen what I consider the most prominent works of each writer, but in the case of Galdós I have chosen instead a little-known short story. Those already familiar with the criticism of John W. Kronik on metafiction in Galdós's novels will understand my choice. Jarnés's *La novia del viento* is another fairly obscure novel that I have included, but it is contrasted with *Locura y muerte de nadie*, perhaps that novelist's most prominent work. Certainly I can be accused of not mentioning novels fully deserving of inclusion within what many conceive as the general category metafiction. In some cases these are conscious omissions on my part responding to the definition I am following; in other cases it may well be that I have failed to recognize a given work's metafictional dimensions, or that I simply do not know the novel in question. I can only hope that I have made enough appropriate selections so as not to skew for the reader the view I am projecting.

When they are readily available I have relied on English

translations of the critical and theoretical works consulted. In the case of the novels analyzed, I have relied exclusively on the Spanish editions but have provided my own translations for every passage cited. For those novels that have been translated I note the English edition in the bibliography.

Although I have published articles on several of the novels analyzed in this study, all the essays here were rewritten for the present book. In most cases the essays here were greatly expanded from the earlier published versions, and in each case they have been refocused to accommodate their role in this study.

Perhaps the students in the Department of Spanish and Portuguese of the University of Kansas who participated in graduate classes with me, particularly those who were in my seminar on metafiction, deserve whatever credit this book may derive, but certainly none of the blame for its defects. In addition to them, several colleagues read sections of the manuscript at various stages of its development, and their always perceptive but never hostile challenges to my ideas have been invaluable. Special thanks are due to Steven Bell, Lucille Kerr, and especially Roberta Spires. I would like to express my appreciation also to the General Research Fund of the University of Kansas for grants enabling me to do the preliminary work on this study and the final editing. For the support to do the primary research and writing I wish to thank the National Endowment for the Humanities, without whose fellowship the task would not have been completed. Finally, I would like to express my gratitude to the staff of the Spencer Research Library at the University of Kansas for providing me with a study in which to do the project.

Introduction

The Metafictional Mode

Several studies of the historical development of metafiction in the European and American novel already exist, the most famous being Robert Alter's *Partial Magic*.[1] Although the subtitle of Alter's book is *The Novel as a Self-Conscious Genre*, he does not attempt to define metafiction's generic or modal components. He offers instead a series of descriptive analyses of self-conscious narration as it appears in works dating from *Don Quijote* to *Pale Fire*. His study, therefore, shows a great deal of metafiction's artistic flexibility but very little of its theoretical basis. His working definition of the concept, however, is important. He defines the self-conscious novel as one that "systematically flaunts its own condition of artifice and that by so doing probes into the problematic relationship between real-seeming artifice and reality" (p. x).

Robert Scholes, in a 1970 article,[2] attempts a much more theoretical discussion of the mode than that proposed by Alter. After first defining four basic fictional forms—romance, novel, myth, and allegory—he establishes four corresponding critical approaches—formal, behavioral, structural, and philosophical. Metafiction, he then concludes, assimilates all the perspectives of criticism into the process itself of fiction. In a later collection of essays on the same subject,[3] Scholes establishes links between the fable and metafiction based on a mutual pleasure in form, authorial dominance, and a didactic quality. Unlike Alter, Scholes does not try to chronicle metafiction but limits himself to analyzing some of the major contemporary works displaying it.

Gustavo Pérez Firmat follows the Scholes's formalist cue to establish a structural connection between the medieval exemplum and metafiction. He argues that both are based on a structural pattern consisting of a brief narration (text) to which the author adds a summary and interpretation of the narration's moral (the scholium). He further refines his definition by proposing two variations of this pattern. In "discursive metafiction" the scholium appears in the form of discursive theorizing about the novel itself, while in "narrative metafiction" the metafictionality of the work depends on an allegorical rendering of characters and events.[4]

In a carefully argued structural approach to the concept of metafiction, Linda Hutcheon defines two basic metafictional modes: diegetically self-aware texts (texts conscious of their own narrative processes) and linguistically self-reflective texts (those foregrounding the limits and the powers of language).[5]

The Meaning of Metafiction is the title of Inger Christensen's recent book in which, beginning with Stern's *Tristram Shandy* and concluding with Beckett's *The Unnameable*, Christensen offers a series of analyses patterned primarily on Wolfgang Kayser's narrative models.[6] For Christensen, metafiction is principally concerned with expressing the novelist's experience by exploring the process of its own making.

Two other books that touch the subject but whose concern is almost exclusively with criticism rather than theory are *The Self-Begetting Novel* by Steven G. Kellman and *The Literature of Exhaustion* by John O. Stark.[7] These two studies contribute in varying degrees to an understanding and definition of metafiction. Yet for my own purposes as a teacher and critic I have found that none of the studies is quite adequate to the task of drawing the limits to what reasonably should and should not be labeled metafiction. Alter, for example, says that a self-conscious novel deliberately exposes the artifice of fiction, which is not to be confused with an elaborately artful novel where the artifice may be prominent. Such a differentiation might be useful if some formula were provided for deciding how "prominent" the artifice must be before it is considered "deliberately exposed." Although Scholes's approach is patterned on formalist-structuralist concepts, his definition of metafiction as a work assimilating all the perspectives of criticism into the process itself of fiction is, if anything, even more open-ended than that of Alter. And Pérez Firmat's "narration-gloss of the narration" formula would seen to allow every novel with an intrusive narrator to qualify as metafiction, while the reliance on allegory for his "narrative metafiction" category threatens to make the term all-inclusive. Even Hutcheon's diegetic versus linguistic categories, which are broken down into overt and covert subcategories, tends to expand the application excessively. Finally, Christensen hardly leads us beyond the now standard definition of metafiction as a novel about itself, a definition that is fine in the most obvious examples where a character or narrator discourses about the nature of novels in general, but inadequate when it is a question of deciding if more subtle and complex techniques qualify as novelistic self-commentary. As a step in the direction of plotting where the limits might be drawn, I have adopted a linguistically grounded approach focused on the concept of modes. And although it is not my intention to propose rigid rules that would force works into narrow categories, I hope that by exploring the concept of metafiction as a fictional mode and by identifying its basic components, I will have contributed to the community effort of better understanding the material we work with.

It is probably fair to say that many literary terms are at best inaccurately defined, primarily because a single term often refers to two related yet different classifications. Realism, for example, has a clear historical identity, yet many contemporary novels are justifiably assigned to that general category. In the case of metafiction the process is reversed. Critics now speak of the *Quijote* and *Tristram Shandy* among other pre-twentieth-century novels as examples of metafiction, yet what is currently becoming recognized as a metafictional movement is generally pinpointed to the decades of the 1960s and 1970s.[8] As is the case with realism and many other terms, metafiction can refer both to historical and to ahistorical classifications. With an eye toward clarifying these two often confusing uses of literary labels and how such uses relate to the term metafiction, some recent work in the field of genres and modes offers itself as a useful point of departure for the present study.

According to Gérard Genette, Plato introduced the word "genre" to literary studies and used it to classify works within historically identifiable traditions. That is, it refers to form in the traditional sense—the distinctions among verse, prose, and drama, but also and more fundamentally among the different types of verse, prose, and drama, e.g., the ode as opposed to the elegiac poem, the pastoral as opposed to the picaresque novel, or Elizabethan as opposed to neoclassical drama. Whatever the criteria employed to make such distinctions—usually some combination of thematics and stylistics—they designate what Plato meant by the term "genre,"[9] or what has commonly come to be labeled literary movement. The essential characteristic of genre or movement in this sense, then, is its identification with a historically defined body of works. "Mode," on the other hand, is a linguistically grounded, synchronic concept: "Modes do not specifically impose a form and are thus prenovelistic: they are applicable to fiction anytime, anywhere."[10]

Ulrich Wicks, for example, the author of the statement cited above, points out that the genre "picaresque novel" has a clear historical identity and is dominated by the picaresque mode; many modern novels offer examples of the picaresque mode, but they should not be confused with the historical group labeled the picaresque novel. Genre and mode, therefore, overlap at the same time that they demand separate consideration and identification. It is probably accurate to say that most, if not all, genres or movements are defined consciously or unconsciously by identifying their modal characteristics along with certain thematic concerns. When the mode is repeated outside the historical boundaries of the genre, however, what results is different from the generic model, notwithstanding the similarities to it. The new context in which it appears changes the whole, even while the mode remains basically constant. For example, within the movement called the Spanish neorealistic novel of the 1940s and 1950s the picaresque mode is prominent in Camilo José Cela's *La familia de Pascual Duarte* (1942) [*The Family of Pascual Duarte* in the English version], while within the New Novel movement of the 1960s the same mode stands out in Juan Marsé's *Ultimas tardes con Teresa* (1966) [*Final Afternoons with Teresa*]. Both novels, however, are radically different from the *Lazarillo*, *El buscón* [*The Swindler* in the English version], and other picaresque novels of the late sixteenth and early seventeenth centuries, as well as from one another. The failure to make the basic distinctions between genre as a diachronic concept and mode as a synchronic concept helps to explain the problems critics have been creating in defining metafiction.[11]

The problem becomes evident if one considers for a moment the fictional mode paradigms proposed not too long ago by Northrop Frye on the one hand and Robert Scholes on the other. In his landmark study, Frye offers the following five fictional modes:

myth: the hero is superior in kind to other men and to his environment.
romance: the hero is superior in degree to other men and to his environment.
high mimetic: the hero is superior in degree to other men but not to his environment.
low mimetic: the hero is superior neither to other men nor to his environment.
irony: the hero is inferior to ourselves.[12]

Various critics have attacked what they point out as the terminological asymmetry of Frye's paradigm.[13] Yet the underlying flaw, as Genette notes in his article, is Frye's confusion between generic and modal criteria. That is to say, Frye sets up his model historically, with the idea that each mode gives way at a particular moment in time to the subsequent mode, a process of evolution culminating in the contemporary era with irony. Frye then implies a circular form as he sees us standing at the threshold of reentrance into the mythic mode. In short, he has applied a generic concept of historical categories to modes, which, as noted, are ahistorical. In addition, by focusing on the nature of the hero he defines modes in basically thematic terms, whereas they are linguistically grounded concepts. Thus by insisting on the hero/other men/environment relationship as the determining factor, what is presented as a modal paradigm is in fact generic; rather than all-inclusive modes, he has created restrictive historical categories. For example, one would assume metafiction to be located in the category of irony. In the cases where the metafictional mode appears, there is probably always an ironic effect, but such an effect cannot be adequately explained by Frye's definition of irony as the hero being inferior to ourselves. Indeed, if he means by "ourselves" the implied reader, in some metafictional examples the "we" is inferior to the so-called hero and to everyone else of the fictional world. In addition, the sequential position of irony as the last item on Frye's paradigm suggests that it is an exclusively contemporary phenomenon, a historical implication belied by works such as the

Quijote and *Tristram Shandy* and a host of others. In summary, as laudable as is Frye's attempt to direct our attention to the concept of modal paradigms, his infelicitous mixture of generic and modal principles predetermines the inadequacy of the system he proposes. Yet what Frye attempts is an important first step, a step to be followed shortly by Robert Scholes's effort to revise the paradigm with the aid of some of his newly acquired structuralist concepts.

Scholes begins by expanding the number of basic modes to seven, and he attempts to correct Frye's terminological asymmetry by relabeling them. Since one of his primary objections to Frye's model concerns its implied circularity and corresponding rigid clockwise progression, Scholes proposes a V-shape graph:

satire   romance
   picaresque   tragedy
      comedy   sentiment
                 history

According to Scholes, both the shape of his graph and the new categories reflect how, from its earliest forms up to the end of the nineteenth century, fiction gravitated from satire and romance toward history. In our present century the process reversed, and he suggests that today we are once again at the top of the graph with novels that are a modal mixture of satire and romance.[14] One of the more attractive features of the model is that, within the general vertical movement, i.e., from picaresque and tragedy to comedy and sentiment, individual authors and works can be plotted horizontally. Dickens's type of realism, for example, might be located near the bottom but to the left, somewhere close to comedy, while Zola's type of naturalism might be pinpointed slightly higher on the scale, leaning toward tragedy. Further distinctions could be made between individual works of the same author: *A Tale of Two Cities* would appear to the right of *Great Expectations* or nearer sentiment, one assumes. Yet in the final analysis Scholes's model falls victim to the same conceptual error as that undermining Frye's: he treats modes as a diachronic phenomenon and defines them in basically thematic terms. The inadequacy of such a mixture of generic and modal concepts becomes evident when one attempts to account for metafiction within Scholes's paradigm. If basically thematic criteria are applied, metafiction can fit everywhere, and from a historical point of view examples of it clearly can be found everywhere. This being the case, one might assume that Scholes does not consider metafiction to be a fictional mode, if it were not for his book *Fabulation and Metafiction*, in which he indicates that it is. The problem, therefore, seems to be with his paradigm rather than with his concept of metafiction, and again the problem with the paradigm can be pinpointed to Scholes's thematic definition of mode.

Notwithstanding the inadequacies of both Frye's and Scholes's attempts to demonstrate graphically the relationships among the various fictional modes, their works still stand as the point of reference for most if not all of the more recent theory on the subject.[15] If both contemporary theory and novelistic practice seem to have passed them by, at least in the case of theory no one has yet offered a viable alternative to their respective paradigms. Since my whole point in raising the issue of fictional modes is to identify metafiction's position among them, I now propose to do so by offering a revision of the Scholes graph (which of course is itself a revision of that offered by Frye). Departing from the basic premise that modes are linguistically grounded concepts and ahistorical, I propose to switch the emphasis from the thematic concern of "better or worse than" to the linguistic process of transforming extratextual reality; rather than constructing a paradigm in which spatial contiguity represents a temporal relationship (satire was followed historically by picaresque and picaresque by comedy, etc.), my groupings are based on similarities in the way fiction transforms extratextual referents. In any one category all historical periods are potentially represented.

Every character, event, and setting in a work of fiction is itself a fiction, even if outside of the fictional text we can identify characters, events, and settings with identical names and seemingly identical characteristics. In short, the word can never be the object to which it refers. Furthermore, the gulf between all language and its point of reference is increased by fiction's quintessential inventiveness, its transformation of extratextual referents into a make-believe world. We can detect the basic nature of the extratextual referent, however, by analyzing the transformed textual simulacrum, for in one way or another the referent leaves its imprint on this transformed image. One method for classifying modes, therefore, is by the nature of the transformed images in a given body of works.

The concept of transformed images can be applied easily to Scholes's categories as he defines them. Satire, he says, represents subhuman grotesqueries enmeshed in chaos, while romance, the mode he places at the same level but as a polar opposite, offers superhuman types in an ideal world. The key words here are "subhuman" and "superhuman," for both make it clear that we are dealing with idiocies or enlightenments. In other words, such transformed images do not carry the imprint of real people and concrete objects from exterior reality, but of abstractions of humanity and the physical world. As he moves down to the next historical level on his graph, Scholes defines picaresque as offering characters in a chaotic world beyond ordinary human tolerance, while tragedy projects heroic figures; however, he insists, the characters and setting of both modes are closer to our own than are those of satire and romance. Stated in terms of referents, then, these modes refer to exaggerated aspects of humanity and nature, but not to total abstractions or concepts. Finally, in comedy he says we find characters with human failings similar to our own, while in sentiment the characters have unheroic virtues to which we may aspire. Imprinted on these fictional images are real types subject to empirical verification; we should be able to imagine, if not recognize, individuals from everyday life who correspond in detail rather than in abstract or exaggerated manners to the fictional model.

The bottom point on the Scholes graph, history, takes us beyond fictional modes. With the historical mode there is no fictionally transformed image, only linguistic markers designed to signify the referent. Furthermore, the referent is supposed to stand the test of scientific rather than merely empirical verification. Since, however, history is not a fictional mode, as Scholes points out, it would seem that it should be just beyond, not at the inverted apex of, the graph. The apex might more logically correspond, therefore, to a mode close to history but still generally identified with fiction: reportorial fiction.[16] Although the referents in this mode are transformed by embellishment into a quasi fictional world, the transformation is minimal; aside from artistic embellishment, the fictional world is supposed to correspond to a documented verification of its referents. Such a fictional mode, standing as it does at the very edge of nonfiction in the form of history, strongly suggests a polar opposite: metafiction, standing at the very edge of nonfiction in the form of novelistic theory. A revision of the Scholes graph, therefore, might begin with a more symmetrical design so as to reflect reportorial fiction and metafiction as polar opposites:

```
                 novelistic theory
        ---------------------------------
                    metafiction
         satire               romance
         picaresque           tragedy
         comedy               sentiment
                 reportorial fiction
        ---------------------------------
                      history
```

By shifting the focus from thematics to the nature of the transformed images, the spatial relationships among categories no longer are designed to represent historical periods. Metafiction and reportorial fiction are furthest apart because of modal differences, not because these two novelistic expressions appeared in completely separated historical periods. Reportorial fiction points almost directly at extratextual reality, while the metafictional mode tends to point back at the work itself. Reportorial texts designate documentally verifiable referents, while the metafictional mode designates fiction itself as the primary referent. In a sense, the language of fictional reporting is transparent since the reader tends to look through it to the designated object, while the language of metafiction tends to be more opaque in that the reader does not look through it so much as at it. Closest to the metafictional mode, then, are satire and romance with their abstract referents. In fact, if we reintegrate Frye's mythic mode (a mode Scholes discards because he feels demons, witches, and animals with supernatural powers should not be compared with humans), we move even closer to the metafictional pole.

Also close to metafiction are the grotesque, which jolts us into an awareness of the fictionality or artificiality of the object,[17] and the fantastic which, according to Todorov, makes us acutely aware of language itself as artifice.[18] Historically, the grotesque and fantastic flourished well after myth, romance, and satire. But by treating them as modes and comparing their modal characteristics to those of myth, romance, and satire, i.e. the radical transformation of the referent, all five can be assigned the same general level on the graph near metafiction. In short, with a modal paradigm in which spatial position is divorced from temporal connotation, it should be possible to account for every fictional mode somewhere between the two poles represented by metafiction and reportorial fiction. In fact, one may choose to draw the line separating fiction from nonfiction before metafiction or reportorial fiction, or indeed to use different labels throughout; the graph is designed to show relative abstract/concrete referents and the two polar axes for fictional modes, not to dictate what is or is not fiction or what labels are most appropriate for a given class of texts.

Finally, a word is in order in reference to the two nonfictional categories, novelistic theory and history. A metafictional mode maintained exclusively throughout a work called a novel, if such were possible, might well cross the line separating fiction from theory. By the same token reportorial fiction, in the opinion of some, crosses the line separating fiction from history. But theory and history themselves can be viewed as fictional or quasi-fictional modes, since both are representations of representations. Even granting such a thesis, the degree of abstraction involved in theory would logically be greater than that involved in history. Although perhaps not as radically distinct as previously viewed, on a modal graph they can be considered polar opposites.

The study of modes, then, requires a putting aside of diachronic considerations inherent in the concept of genre or movement. Yet, as the connotation of the verbal construct "putting aside" suggests, responsible critics cannot afford to ignore completely the problem of historical categories. In spite of the problems Frye and Scholes create for themselves by mixing modal and generic criteria in their respective paradigms, obviously there is a complex overlapping between genre and mode that needs to be confronted. Literary styles and movements follow historical patterns and tend to repeat themselves—therefore Frye's circular and Scholes's vertical explanations.

There is a basic fallacy, however, in both explanations even when limited to genres. For, whereas it is true that literary forms tend to repeat themselves, the repetitions do not follow rigid patterns but are only partial, or repetitions with variations. Myths are being written today, but we recognize them as much by their differences from as by their similarities to the ancient models. In short, by way of a visual image of the relationship between modes and the historical process of genres, we can imagine a series of connecting coils, as in a spring, positioned within the rectangular pattern formed by my modal categories. Then, rather than Scholes's concept of exclusively vertical movement, fiction can be imagined as descending and ascending in a spiral, its movement both vertical and horizontal. The points touched while ascending would never be identical to those touched while descending. The coil spring analogy reflects the impossibility of a genre ever being repeated in exact form, for in its spiral movement the modal combinations are constantly changing and in so doing are giving birth to new, if somewhat similar, movements. Thus the visual image of the modal paradigm framing the coil spring is offered to reflect how these combinations represent structures of difference from previous genres. And the structures of difference, whether merely intuited or carefully analyzed, perhaps explain the constant creation of new generic categories, both by novelists who reply to previous novelists by means of the novels they write, and by critics who identify the resulting characteristics and label the categories. Metafiction stands prominently as one of the more recent examples of a new generic category. As a movement it has only recently emerged, but the metafictional mode can be traced back to the earliest examples of what we call novels.

One theoretical concept that is central to my study should be clarified here: the use of the term reader. In spite of the plethora in recent years of reader and reader-response theories, too often no clear distinction is made among what I see as three distinct dimensions of narrative discourse: the text reader, the text-act reader, and the real reader. First of all, there are readers within the text, addressees to whom a narrator directs his or her discourses—the text readers. The most obvious example of such a text reader occurs in epistolary novels in which the fictional letters are addressed to a specified recipient who may or may not ever appear in person, or the *Vuestra Merced* invoked in such picaresque novels as the *Lazarillo* and *El Buscón*. But even if the addressee is not identified, for each narrative voice there is an implicit recipient enclosed, as is the speaker, within the text. The text reader, therefore, is a purely linguistic dimension of the text. And whereas the identified text reader is also a verbal construct, the non-identified, non-explicitly-characterized text reader is a part of the general construct of discourse itself.

Just as there is a recipient, implicit or explicit, for each voice within the text, there is a recipient, normally implicit but as we shall see sometimes explicit, for the sum total of the work's voices. By way of clarification, within the novelistic world there may be any number of text-speech acts each with its own sender and receiver. Beyond the novelistic world, nevertheless, there is a single, normally implied, sender or creator (Booth's implied author) of all the individual text-speech acts; also beyond the novelistic world, therefore, is a single, normally implied, receiver of all the individual text-speech acts: the text-act reader. (Although one might object to the somewhat awkward term "text-act reader" when one has at one's disposal Iser's popular "implied reader," as the preceding argument has tried to demonstrate, both the recipient embedded within the novelistic world and the one stationed outside it may be implied.) And whereas the context of the text recipients is the novelistic world in which they are embedded, the context of the text-act reader is the sociohistorical world in which the work is created.

Finally, there is the real reader who consciously or subconsciously projects him- or herself into the role of the text-act reader so as to apprehend as accurately as possible the text's message. But such a projection can never be accomplished totally; the novel's message can never be apprehended completely. Working against the real reader and his or her efforts to assume the role of text-act reader are language itself and the impossibility of reducing it to a univocal statement, an impossibility that most literary works consciously exploit. Furthermore, since the real reader's text is not only the written work but the written work viewed within its sociohistorical context, there is the eternal question concerning what aspects of the context to consider. And the aspects we focus on, both within the written work and outside of it, respond also to many factors, one of which is our own sociohistorical context. That is to say, our present context influences the way we read. In addition, the reading we give the work will depend on our critical strategies and competencies. As a result, not only will there be at least some difference between any two people's readings, but any one person's readings will be altered according to his or her ever changing sociohistorical context, to the critical strategies he or she employs, and to the competencies and expectations he or she develops.

It should be noted, furthermore, that in the case of basically representational or mimetic fiction written more or less at the time of the reading, all three readers (text, text-act, and real) seem to be one and the same. They are not, but since the differences are not pronounced we have the illusion that they are identical and that the written text directly mirrors reality. In the case of irony, on the other hand, the difference between text reader and text-act reader may become dramatic. In *La familia de Pascual Duarte*, for example, when the transcriber swears he has not changed a thing in the manuscript but has cut out some objectionable sections that might be harmful to the reader's moral health, the message he directs to his text reader is radically different from that directed to the text-act reader. So literature of the fantastic, science fiction, or novels with historical settings mark dramatic differences between the text reader or readers and the text-act reader. As temporal (or cultural) differences between the writing and the reading increase, the real reader may find the task of projecting him- or herself into the role of the text-act reader increasingly difficult, requiring in some cases special historical-cultural background orientation in order even to attempt such a projection. For the text recipient, then, the text is that contained within the written artifact. For the text-act reader the text is that within the artifact plus the context in which it was written. And for the real reader the text is that within the artifact plus the context in which it was written plus his or her own context at the moment of reading.

When in this study I speak of the text reader and the text-act reader, therefore, I will be referring to an inherent dimension of all fictional discourse, the first embedded within the fictitious world and the second separate from it. When I refer, on the other hand, to the real reader or when I speak of the reader's (or our) reaction to a given passage, I am not implying anything more than my attempt to project myself into the role of the text-act reader; in no way do I mean to suggest some type of absolute knowledge as to how others may react, or that such a reaction is the appropriate reaction elicited. Indeed, at best my ability to project myself into the role of the text-act reader will be limited, and my reading will be to one degree or another a misreading. I can only hope that such a misreading serves to open the text in question to yet other readers equipped with yet other critical strategies and further developed expectations and competencies.[19]

Now that I have proposed metafiction's definition relative to other fictional modes, and my reader categories, I would like to focus more directly on its modal components. The point of departure for such a focus will be Gérard Genette's landmark contribution to the theory of fiction, *Narrative Discourse*. Genette, echoing Benveniste's term "instances de discours,"[20] defines narrative mode as the "situation d'énonciation" or the act of narrating.[21] The act of narrating involves the participants (narrator and narratee), the context, and the extratextual referent. The act of narrating, moreover, is normally implicitly rather than explicitly stated in the narrative. Whereas to this point the focus has been on the concept of the referent imprinted on the images of the text, now it will be on the fictional speech act imprinted on the narrative discourse.

The concept of the act of narrating as imprinted on the narrative discourse evolves from Genette's thesis that there are two basic levels or worlds in the fictional text: "the world in which one tells and the world of which which one tells" (*Discourse*, p. 236). Since the world *in* which one tells normally is not directly revealed, it must be constructed by the "traces it has left—the traces it is considered to have left—in the narrative discourse it is considered to have produced" (*Discourse*, p. 214). Even in the case where the fictional act of narrating is revealed—epistolary novels, for instance—there is still another hidden level of the act of narrating involving the implied author.

The world *of* which one tells, then, is the product of the act of narrating, it is the story, or the "what of narrative."[22] The level of the world of the story is the primary if not exclusive focus of attention for the casual or uninitiated reader, even in the case of fictitious memoirs. If within this second level of the story a character relates an ancedote or presents a narrative document, the text's narrative levels double. The character is now a narrator corresponding to a third narrative level, and his product or story corresponds to what would be a fourth narrative level.[23] As more stories are embedded within stories, additional narrative levels are created and result in a "Chinese box" effect. However many levels are involved, "The transition from one narrative level to another can in principle be achieved only by the narrating, the act that consists precisely of introducing into one situation, by means of a discourse, the knowledge of another situation" (*Discourse*, p. 234). If, therefore, a narrator, narratee, or character from one level intrudes into another, he or she violates the conventions of fiction, producing, according to Genette, an effect of strangeness that is either comical or fantastic.[24] Such an explanation of narrative levels and how they can be violated is an important step toward defining the metafictional mode. A modification must be made, however, before we can arrive at an adequate definition: in addition to the world *from* which one speaks and the world *of* which one speaks, the fictional mode is constituted by the world from which one listens or reads.[25]

When Genette mentions the narratee, he places him on the same level or within the same world as the speaker; that is, the narratee corresponds to what I defined above as the text reader. Yet Genette's two-world explanation does not accommodate the addressee for the sum total of all the text speaker/reader combinations: the text-act reader. Just as there is an implied author who is the creator of all narrators, so there is an implied text-act reader to whom he addresses himself. And whereas the addressee within the speaker's world may be implied, he also may be a character and therefore capable of responding. According to the conventions of fiction, the addressee of the entire narrative does not enjoy such a capacity; he exists, therefore, in a separate world, a world as sacred to the conventions of fiction as are those of the fictive author and the story.

If we accept the fictional mode as a triad consisting of the world of the fictive author, the world of the story, and the world of the text-act reader—subject of course to interior duplication by means of embedded stories—a metafictional mode results when the member of one world violates the world of another. Such a violation might involve a character from the world of the story challenging the authority of the fictive author, or the fictive author asking advice of the text-act reader, or the members of all three worlds engaging in direct discourse with one another. Such violations of the boundaries separating these three worlds, boundaries that have come to be accepted as sacred conventions of fiction, call attention to the arbitrariness of the conventions and thereby unmask any illusion that what is being narrated is real rather than mere fiction. Yet there is a certain contradiction in this whole process. When the world of, say, the fictive author is violated and he is thereby made an explicit part of the fiction, standing beyond him is always another implied or fictive author. The same is true with the text-act reader, for once he is dramatized into the fiction there has to be another text-act reader to whom that dramatizing process is addressed. In the final analysis, therefore, metafiction violates one set of modes merely to replace it with another.[26] Metafiction cannot escape its own prison-house of fiction.

What I have been proposing up to this point is a definition of the metafictional mode. Such a mode has given rise within the last decade or so to what I think is now generally recognized as a metafictional movement. In the case of the Spanish version appearing in the 1790s and early 1980s, the emphasis has shifted from unmasking the conventions to foregrounding the process of creating fiction; rather than a narrator, reader, or character violating another's boundaries, there is a violation of the traditional distinctions among the act of narrating, the act of reading, and the narrated product. The focus, therefore, is no longer directed exclusively or even primarily to the world of the story, but rather to the process of creating the story, either through the act of writing or through the act of reading. In other cases the acts of writing and reading are supplanted by discourse among the characters; the story in effect consists of a discussion of how to write the work of fiction, how to create a novel to enclose the discourse. And although again it is a question of exchanging one type of illusion for another, no longer is the effect merely one of strangeness as the artifices and conventions of fiction are exposed, for here the novel focuses on its own coming-into-being. No longer does the novel merely tend to point back at itself; now it points primarily at itself.

In order to distinguish between the metafictional mode and this movement that has evolved from it, I have chosen to call the latter the self- referential novel. This new novelistic expression is the product of the spiral evolution proposed above in which at a given moment one mode surges to the foreground to give rise to a new movement while, with the next step in the vertical-horizontal progression of the spiral, that mode fades to the background and a new mode is featured. Yet in this spiral progression traces from the previously foregrounded modes infiltrate the one presently dominating, producing in the process an infinite series of unique yet familiar novelistic expressions.

The Spanish self-referential novel is an example of such an expression of the metafictional mode. In the following chapter I will begin the process of tracing metafiction's evolution from mode to this current movement by looking at three pre-twentieth century precursors.

Chapter One

Violations and Pseudo-Violations: *Quijote, Buscón,* and "La novela en el tranvía"

As I begin this examination of the precursors of the Spanish metafictional mode with works of Cervantes, Quevedo, and Galdós, I confess to a certain inhibition upon entering such well charted waters. I feel compelled to emphasize, therefore, that my analyses of the *Quijote* and *Buscón* will be limited to those episodes featuring the metafictional mode; only in the case of the Galdós short story do I attempt anything resembling a complete reading. The analyses in this chapter are designed to demonstrate and thereby clarify the concept of violation—the textual strategy of breaking the arbitrary conventions of fiction. By examining these early and somewhat tentative violations of the laws of fiction, I hope to demonstrate how the contemporary novels, although more radical in the strategies they employ, carry the imprint of the earlier models.[1] The metafictional mode, to repeat the thesis proposed in the Introduction, transcends historical classifications.

Critics of almost every persuasion, ranging from Américo Castro to Dorothy Van Ghent, from José Ortega y Gasset to Wolfgang Kayser, have found justification for labeling the *Quijote* the first modern novel.[2] Little wonder, therefore, that Robert Alter also found Cervantes' masterpiece an indispensable point of departure for his historical survey of self-conscious narration.[3] Notwithstanding the possible objection that I am merely following Alter's footsteps by beginning my analyses with the same novel, I think there is enough contrast between our approaches to minimize any sense of tautology.

Without much question the most celebrated example in the

Quijote involving a violation of the boundaries separating the three fictional worlds is the battle in Part One between the novel's protagonist and the Biscayan. As most will recall, the narrator is describing the two combatants with swords raised and shields firmly grasped when he suddenly interrupts his narrative to announce that the account ends here because the "first author" could not find the concluding section of the manuscript. Such a dramatic switch from the story to the act of narrating constitutes an obvious violation of the conventions of fiction. Yet even more blatant is the violation committed by the narrator when he evokes the role of the first author and places the blame on him for the truncation of the story. The narrator, as the subordinate of the first author, is in effect rebelling against his superior. Furthermore, the narrator transgresses the boundary separating the two when, after expressing his irritation at such an inopportune truncation, he usurps the first author's authority and sets out on his own to find the missing documents.

That the continuation of a story depends on locating the missing manuscript challenges, of course, the assumption of authorship established in the prologue and in the famous initial sentence of the novel: "En un lugar de la Mancha de cuyo nombre no quiero acordarme"[4] ["In a place in the Mancha whose name I prefer to forget"]. With the intrusion of the narrator or self-defined "second author" to explain that the "first author" (a Moorish historian named Cide Hamete Benengeli) could not find the remaining manuscript, the identity of the "I" with which the novel begins must be questioned retrospectively. Since the "second author" in effect is only an author when he narrates the search, and otherwise is merely a transcriber, and Cide Hamete as a historian is supposedly also only a combination translator-transcriber, and the anonymous author may in fact be a community of authors, none seems to qualify as the "I" of the narrating act. Indeed, the problem of the source of authority is further complicated when the "second author," after finally discovering the documents, hires someone to translate them from Arabic to Spanish. Not only does the emergence of a second translator raise the question of this translator's fidelity to the original text, but the second translator also becomes an author when, in Part Two, at the beginnings of chapters 5, 24, and 27, he questions the verisimilitude of Sancho's conversation with his wife, calls attention to the first author's marginal notes, and offers an explanation of the Moorish historian's use of a Catholic oath. As a result of the confusion over who is actually speaking and with what narrative authority or veracity, the boundary separating the primary speaker from the subordinate speakers is completely blurred.

As is evident in the preceding explanation, the whole story of Don Quijote and Sancho seems to depend on someone other than the voice heard at the novel's beginning. Indeed, not only our confidence in, but the very textual existence of, the anonymous author or authors depends on Cide Hamete's transcription, which in turn depends on the transcription and successful search for the manuscript by the "second author," and finally on the assumption that the translation of it is punctilious. Yet paradoxically none of these supposedly subordinate speakers (Cide Hamete, the "second author," and the translator) would exist if it were not for the story of the knight and his squire as told by the anonymous author or authors of the manuscript, for these speakers are textual extensions of this narration. Such conflicts of authority, created when subordinate speakers violate the boundary separating them from the primary speaker, function as a textual strategy for directing attention to the arbitrary conventions of all fictional authority. As a result, the focus switches from the illusion to the artifices responsible for creating the illusion. The fictionality of fiction is thus foregrounded, and such a foregrounding reveals that within the text there are not authors but only fictitious figures disguised as authors.

Not content with revealing that authors within a text are mere fictions, Cervantes in Book Two explores the fictionality of the reader. The focus on the world of the text-act reader occurs when a student tells Don Quijote and Sancho about the book he has just read entitled *El Ingenioso Hidalgo don Quijote de la Mancha* by Cide Hamete Benengeli. As the two protagonists then question the young scholar about their respective projected images in the book, the conversation serves as a critique of Part One. Since, however, the critique consists of fictitious characters contemplating themselves as fictitious characters, they have transgressed the boundary separating the world in which characters perform from the world in which they are seen performing. Don Quijote and Sancho are therefore readers of their own story, albeit the student stands between them and the written text. They are readers, that is to say, in the oral or *juglar* sense of the word.

The characters themselves, nevertheless, do not consider what they are contemplating to be fictitious. On the contrary, for them the book is a historical record of their exploits, and their primary concern is with the accuracy of the account, especially in view of the Moorish nationality of the author Cide Hamete (Moors are notorious liars, according to Don Quijote). Yet as the discussion continues, Don Quijote as reader-protagonist discovers that his story is best served by poetic rather than historical truth.

The issue of historical versus poetic truth arises when the student, described upon his introduction into the novel as "de condición maliciosa y amigo de donaires y de burlas" (2.3:67) ["of a malicious disposition and very fond of plays on words and practical jokes"], begins to bait the two reader-protagonists. He states, for example, that some people have criticized the book for detailing every one of the physical abuses Don Quijote suffers. The student adds to this affront to Don Quijote's dignity by noting that, since the account of so many beatings becomes farcical, poetic license could easily be exercised. Don Quijote, although far from admitting that his story is a farce, welcomes the suggestion of poetic license, arguing that the author indeed could have omitted some of the incidents without altering the basic truth of the story. After all, he reasons, Aeneas certainly was not as pious as Virgil represented him, nor Ulysses as prudent as Homer indicated. At this point the student does an about-face and argues that historians cannot add or delete anything without compromising the veracity of their accounts; poets, on the other hand, enjoy the freedom to write of things as they should be.

While the malicious motive for the student's critical maneuvering seems obvious, Don Quijote's sudden espousal of poetic over historical truth is more complex. First and foremost, of course, would be his attempt to recapture his dignity, and significantly his first justification for omitting some of the painful incidents is fairness—"equidad" (2.3:71). But there are also indications of more complex psychological processes within the protagonist, processes which in turn have theoretical implications vis-à-vis the work of fiction. When he compares his situation to those of Aeneas and Ulysses, he is identifying with fictitious personages, an identification even more dramatically evident later in the Maese Pedro puppet show episode. But the self he is thus identifying here is his literary self, the self recreated by the student's oral discourse. It is not strange, therefore, that he should compare that verbal construct with other verbal constructs from oral literary tradition. In other words, he is drawing a clear distinction between the verbal representation of him by others and the self that now is the recipient of such a representation. Don Quijote exists at this point simultaneously as actor and audience. And his role as audience, as reader of his own verbal image, allows him to see that the verbal image can never *be* the thing it represents, the word can never become the object. Little wonder, therefore, that he appeals to poetic license, for now he at least senses—is forced to sense by virtue of the student's maliciously inspired stratagem—that even historical representation is an illusion, a fiction of the reality it pretends to be. And of course we the real readers now have the opportunity to contemplate—by virtue of Cervantes' textual stratagem—how fiction is the vehicle par excellence for displaying language's illusory essence.

The key to recognizing any illusion is recognition of the devices that create it or, in the game of fiction, recognition of the conventions by which the game is played. When Don Quijote listens to and comments on the published account of his misadventures and thereby becomes his own reader, he points not only at the fictionality of the novel's ancedote but at the convention that hides the recipient from view. By violating the boundary between the world in which he performs and the world from which he is seen performing, he draws attention to the text-act reader as an integral element of the fictional mode, or to borrow an expression from Walter Ong, he alerts us to the fact that indeed "The Writer's Audience Is Always a Fiction."[5] But at the same time that the world of the text-act reader is invaded, another world is automatically created to replace it; if Don Quijote is now standing where the text-act reader was stationed, the latter is now one step back. A violation exposes but does not destroy the fictional mode. And since every real reader, consciously or subconsciously, attempts to identify with the text-act reader, we stand just behind Don Quijote as he contemplates the conventions that create illusion: the illusion that language is what it represents, that fiction is reality.

In fact, the laying bare of illusion is the motive Cide Hamete himself professes at the end of the novel: "pues no ha sido otro mi deseo de poner en aborrecimiento de los hombres las fingidas y disparatadas historias de los libros de caballerías" (2.74:353) ["For my sole object has been to arouse man's contempt for the false and absurd stories of chivalric novels"]. Yet his professed motive is itself subject to being laid bare. Since within the fiction there is an anonymous author or authors of Don Quijote's and Sancho's story, and since Cide Hamete is merely one of the transcribers, in the final analysis Cide Hamete is but one more reader of the story, as are the "second author," the translator, and Don Quijote himself. Cide Hamete's professed intent, therefore, has no more inherent textual authority than the statements of any other of these readers pretending to be authors. In fact, one "reading" suggested by this textual strategy is that in the final analysis all authors are merely readers expressing their reading in graphic form. For every apparent creative source there is a prior creative source. Final meaning, therefore, is always deferred to an infinite future of yet another reading. In the most profound sense of the word the *Quijote* is, as has been noted before, a novel about reading novels.[6]

It would be inadequate and something of a distortion to categorize the *Quijote* as merely a metafictional novel. The metafictional is one of many modes that play an important role in the novel.[7] Indeed, the modal complexity of the *Quijote* may well explain why the novel continues to attract the attention of virtually each new critical school.

The violations of the boundaries separating the three worlds of the fictional mode in the *Quijote* direct attention to the artifices of fiction. A mere appearance of a violation, on the other hand, can serve as a quite different textual strategy. Any threat to the boundaries between fictional worlds creates tension and thereby emphasizes the textual context in which the threat occurs. If the threat ends in a true violation the effect is metafictional; however, if the threat is never realized, or only tentatively realized, the artifices remain hidden and attention is fixed on the episode or passage in which the indication of a violation occurs. *El Buscón* [*The Swindler* in the English version] offers a very good example of a borderline violation whose effect is emphatic but not metafictional. Such an example should help clarify the basic definition of metafiction which has been proposed in this study.

The episode concerns chapter VII of Part II, one of the key chapters of the novel for it marks a definitive downward turn in the picaro's moral and material well-being. The incident in question involves the scheme of the protagonist/narrator Pablos to marry into a wealthy family by convincing the members that he is Don Felipe Tristán, a nobleman and heir to an estate. His strategy seems to be working to perfection until his former master, Don Diego, arrives on the scene. Pablos had served Don Diego when both were students and their relationship was, or so Pablos thought, that of friends rather than servant to master. In spite of the years that have passed, Don Diego immediately suspects that the supposed Don Felipe Tristán is in reality Pablos. When Pablos denies his true identity, Don Diego insults him by begging forgiveness for having mistaken a gentleman for someone as amoral and vile as his former servant. To this insult is added humiliation when the next day, in the presence of his fiancée and Don Diego, Pablos is thrown from a horse he had borrowed without the owner's knowledge. He is further embarrassed when the owner suddenly appears to claim his horse. This episode inspires Don Diego to investigate the motive and confirm the identity of the disguised Pablos, and after having done so, to devise a plan for two thugs to attack and brutally beat the poor imposter.

The apparent violation of narrative level involves Don Diego's investigations and his plots to ambush Pablos. Since Pablos as the first-person narrator naturally was not a witness to these acts of espionage and plots for ambush directed against him, his narration of them could only be by means of someone else's accounts. Yet not only does he fail to identify the sources of his information, but as he narrates the beating he seems to contradict his own previous narrative account: "pero nunca sospeché en don Diego ni en lo que era"[8] ["but I never suspected Don Diego nor what was going on"]. In spite of the apparent contradiction, the preterite tense, "sospeché," indicates that the point of focalization is from the protagonist in the past and not from the narrator in his narrative present. That is to say, at the time the beating occurred Pablos never even suspected Don Diego; from his narrative position now, however, he obviously knows differently, as the narration of the plot against him clearly indicates. By focalizing that moment of the beating from the experiencing self's perspective,[9] Pablos's naive confidence in his former friend's fidelity is juxtaposed with that former friend's treachery.

As this example demonstrates, a tentative or partial violation directs attention to the episode rather than to fiction's artifices. Indeed, since Pablos directs his narrative to a text reader identified as *vuestra merced* (or *v.m.* as he is labeled in the text), this text reader might well here question his addresser's reliability. The message to the text-act reader, however, does not concern reliability but a so-called nobleman's sense of honor. As a representative of the noble class Don Diego reveals that his sense of honor is just as corrupt as that of a picaro.[10] Since the text reader's title, *vuestra merced*, identifies him as also a member of the noble class, he is guilty by association. Thus Pablos is not really talking *to* but *about* his text reader; his message assumes a recipient distanced from the world of the story. In a fashion similar to what happens in the *Lazarillo*, *vuestra merced* is a part of rather than the intended recipient of the text-act message. In short, Pablos is very much in control of the narrating act as he subtly attacks his own text reader. And since no laws of fiction are actually violated, this is not a case of metafiction but of a textual strategy designed to emphasize a tragic turning point in the fictional life of the protagonist. This distinction between violation and apparent violation is fundamental to my definition of metafiction. There is reason to believe that Quevedo, consummate artist that he was, consciously bent, but without breaking, the fictional mode so as to achieve the effect he wanted.

For the final examples demonstrating the metafictional mode in pre-twentieth-century texts, I will jump from the seventeenth to the nineteenth century and focus on the great Spanish realist novelist Benito Pérez Galdós. (Since in the history of Spanish fiction the eighteenth century is not particularly significant, such a leap is less extreme than it may appear at first glance.) Considering Robert Alter's thesis that the nineteenth century is a period of eclipse for self-conscious narration,[11] it may come as a surprise that Galdós not only is an exception but deserves credit as a true innovator in strategies for violating the conventions of fiction. John W. Kronik has analyzed with uncommon insight three novels of Don Benito in which a character violates the world of the fictive author. In *El amigo Manso* (1882) [*Good Friend Manso*] the protagonist, by declaring at the novel's very beginning that he does not exist, also in so doing declares his autonomy from the fictive author; the protagonist claims credit for his own eventual development into a character, whereas the other characters, as Kronik demonstrates, are products of the fictive author.[12]

The violation of the fictive author's world is even bolder in *Misericordia* (1897) [*Piety*]. In this case the protagonist invents a priest to explain how she gets the money to sustain her mistress, and one day the priest miraculously materializes. As Kronik demonstrates, we have here an example of a character creating another character and in so doing usurping the creative prerogative of the fictive author.[13] In yet another example of characters usurping the creative function of the fictive author, Kronik explores the way in which the protagonist Fortunata of the novel *Fortunata y Jacinta* is in effect the product of some half dozen characters who collaborate in her creation.[14] *La de Bringas* (1884) [*The Spendthrifts* in the English version], on the other hand, offers another type of violation, in this case the fictive author transgressing the world of the story. The most humorous example of such a transgression occurs at the novel's end. After having chronicled Rosalía de Bringas's obsession with material possessions, her desperate attempts to pay her debts, her husband's dismissal from his bureaucratic position in the government, and finally the compromise of her honor in a futile attempt to enlist the aid of a family friend in her economic crisis, the omniscient narrator suddenly appears in the protagonist's world. He says that shortly after the affair with the family friend, he had his own encounter with Rosalía: "Quiso repetir las pruebas de su ruinosa amistad, mas yo me apresuré a ponerles punto, pues si parecía natural que ella fuese el sostén de la cesante familia, no me creía yo en el caso de serlo, contra todos los fueros de la moral y de la economía doméstica"[15] ["She tried to repeat the experience of her disastrous episode with the family friend, but I hastened to head her off, for whereas it seemed fine for her to serve as the provider for her unemployed spouse and her family, I didn't feel it was my place to play the same role, in respect to both moral and economical dicta"].

The preceding examples demonstrate that Galdós, whether consciously or unconsciously, is a disciple of the Cervantes model, and possibly those of Stern, Fielding, and others, for violating the conventions of fiction. His strategies, although certainly more than mere imitations of his predecessors, carry the imprint of the earlier models. Yet one of his first efforts in writing fiction, a short story entitled "La novela en el tranvía" (1871) ["The Streetcar Novel"], seems to suggest that he also learned from the Quevedo model. This story offers an example of a violation of narrative level and then a negation of the violation. Such a backing away from a metafictional focus underscores some of the inherent contradictions in the realistic mode of which Galdós was to become Spain's most celebrated master.[16]

The story is a first-person narrative in which the protagonist/narrator meets a friend on a streetcar. The friend, an incurable gossip, begins telling about a conflict involving a countess, a count, and a young man who has a close but platonic relationship with the countess. The conflict is orchestrated by the household's majordomo who, if successful in his evil machinations designed to lead the count into a crime of passion, hopes to gain control of the family estate. But before the friend can finish the narrative he reaches his destination and departs. The protagonist/narrator then glances at the newspaper serving as a wrapping for some books he is returning to another friend, and discovers the same story of the countess appearing there as a fictitious serial. Again, however, the story is truncated before the denouement, this time by a cut in the newspaper made by the protagonist when he wrapped the books. After his surprise at what he thought was a true story turning out to be fictitious, he is even more astonished when the reverse occurs: seated directly across from him now is the majordomo of the serial story.

The events have now taken a fantastic turn since the protagonist/narrator really believes he is observing in the flesh a fictional being: "novelesco, inverosímil, convertido en ser vivo y compañero mío en aquel viaje" (p. 507) ["novelistic, non-verisimilar, transformed into a living being and my companion on that trip"]. Fiction has become reality. Of course, this is merely another game of illusion created by the intrusion of a character from the fourth narrative level into the second narrative level. To clarify, the first narrative level corresponds to the narrating self as he tells his story: "y lo creí como ahora creo que es pluma esto con que escribo" (p. 514) ["I believed it just as now I believe that this thing with which I am writing is a pen"]. The second level, then, corresponds to his narrated experiences on the streetcar. Within this second level, however, first the friend and then the anonymous narrator of the serial tell their respective stories (really the same story), so their act of narrating constitutes the third narrative level. Finally, the fourth level corresponds to the world of which they speak, or the conflict involving the countess, the count, the young man, and the evil majordomo—the latter now apparently sitting on the streetcar of level two. If we had only the friend's incomplete story, the appearance of the majordomo would be merely fortuitous; since we also have the fictitious serial, his appearance is fantastic. With this blurring of the boundaries between fact and fiction, between the second and fourth narrative levels, the rules of the game of fiction are placed in a state of suspension. The protagonist/narrator's "reality" is counterpoised by the majordomo's "fictionality." The two men are now equally real or equally fictitious. The conventions of fiction are suddenly laid bare.

With the conventions now in a state of suspension, the protagonist/narrator feels justified in committing his own violation of narrative level when the majordomo disembarks after first sinisterly examining a letter he is carrying: "Cuando salió el hombre en quien creí ver al terrible mayordomo, me quedé pensando en el incidente de la carta, y me lo expliqué a mi manera, no queriendo ser, en tan delicada cuestión, menos fecundo que el novelista, autor de lo que momentos antes había leído" (p. 507) ["When the man I thought was the terrible majordomo got off, I continued to think about the incident of the letter, and I explained it in my own way, not wishing to be less creative in such a delicate matter than the novelist, the author of what I had read moments before"]. When the protagonist/narrator assumes the responsibility for continuing the story, he violates the third narrative level corresponding to the serial's author; he usurps that author's position and plagiarizes his story material. Yet at this moment of maximum invasion of narrative levels, the seeds are planted to reaffirm the boundaries and negate the apparent violations. Such a restorative process is initiated with the words from the quoted passage, "el hombre en quien creí ver." Both the verb and its tense mark a difference between the narrating self corresponding to the first level and the experiencing self of the second level. The narrating self is now implying by his use of this verb form that rather than a case of fiction becoming reality, his experiencing self was at the time a victim of self-delusion.

The process of restoring the boundaries between narrative levels—and between "reality" and "fiction"—continues when the protagonist/narrator falls asleep and furthers the countess's story in a dream. Even though his dreaming self corresponds to the third narrative level (or the level corresponding to the friend who began the tale and the serial that continued it), and that which is dreamed to the fourth level, in this case there is no violation, merely a narrated switch in narrative level. And of course since we know he is dreaming, the boundary between "reality" and "fiction" remains intact.

Although the dream extends the story to the point where the count seems about to commit his crime of passion, the protagonist/narrator is awakened before the climactic moment. He then hears a conversation on the streetcar between someone he believes to be the young man of the story and a fellow traveler, and the conversation appears to concern the countess's fate. But when the two young men are about to disembark and the protagonist/narrator interrupts them to ask how the countess dies, they break into laughter and leave. Immediately after their departure a woman gets on with a dog matching the vision of the countess's dog in his dream. Under his questioning she confirms that indeed the dog's mistress has just died, but when he then asks what happened to the count, she laughs and calls him a madman. Then three men get on the streetcar talking about the shooting death of a hapless female victim. Rather than the countess, however, he learns that the victim was their hunting dog. Finally, he again sees the supposed majordomo, attacks him, is arrested, discovers that the man is a respected businessman, and ends the story by admitting that several months passed before he regained his sanity. "Reality" thus reconquers "fiction" and the boundaries between the narrative levels are reaffirmed. All the violations are explained as the protagonist/narrator's illusion.

The strategy of violating and then negating the violations of narrative levels underscores even more the eternal conflict between reality and fiction, truth and illusion. Galdós in this story manipulates the text-act reader into first questioning the very conventions that allow fiction to seem real, and then reaccepting them. When the protagonist/narrator confesses at the end that he was insane at the time he thought the fictitious characters had come to life, the text-act reader should retrospectively dismiss those transformations as illusions. Reality, therefore, comes with the protagonist/narrator's recognition that the characters were "real people" only resembling the creations of his imagination. (Obviously such a reality is itself an illusion, another fiction made to seem real by the conventions of fiction.) The violation-negation strategy in the final analysis draws attention to the paradox of fiction's reality and to the inexorable attraction of its illusions.

The strategy also addresses another dimension of the relationship between fiction and reality, that of the referents. The question of referents is crystalized when the protagonist/narrator is at the edge of sleep and begins considering the influences on his thoughts: "Yo, que he leído muchas y muy malas novelas, di aquel giro a la que, insensiblemente, iba desarrollándose en mi imaginación por las palabras de un amigo, la lectura de un trozo de papel y la vista de un desconocido" (p. 508) ["I, who have read many, and some very bad, novels, tossed around what, unconsciously, was taking form in my imagination thanks to a friend's words, the reading of a section from a newspaper, and the sight of a stranger"]. This passage underscores the complexity of artistic sources for any novelist. In addition to empirically observing his social reality, the realist also borrows, consciously or unconsciously, from what he hears and reads, including fictitious accounts. In view of this borrowing, one can say, as Pirandello later would, that characters search for their own author; whether the author realizes it or not, every work of literature is but one more link in a complex network of literary intertextuality. By means of his manipulation of the metafictional mode in "La novela en el tranvía," Galdós displays at a very early age a full awareness that realism refers to literature as well as to social reality. The violation-negation strategy, therefore, allows him to display both of these fundamental dimensions of his craft. It is not without irony that Spain's greatest realist novelist was perhaps his century's most blatant violator of the conventions designed to make fiction seem real. Indeed, it is tempting to speculate that Galdós felt it his personal obligation to expose the inherent contradiction in labeling any type of fiction "realism."

One more word is in order in reference to Galdós and metafiction. His type of modal violations should not be confused with what is commonly labeled the intrusive or editorial narrator. Whereas it is true that an intrusive or editorial narrator interrupts his narrative and thereby calls attention to his own presence, he does not, at least in the typical nineteenth-century realist novel, direct attention to the artifices of fiction. On the contrary, the sententious nature of most such intrusions directs attention from the work to extratextual reality. Interrupting editorial comments aimed at the nature of what has been narrated or how it has been narrated, on the other hand, represent the type of self-consciousness generally labeled metafiction.[17]

The metafictional mode, as argued in the Introduction and demonstrated in this chapter, is an atemporal textual strategy involving a violation of the conventions of fiction. In the *Quijote*, considered by many as the first modern novel, the violations concern authorial source and the sanctity of the text-reader's world, as well as that of the characters (the appearance in the *Quijote* of a character from the plagiarized version of the novel). Notwithstanding the prominence of the mode in Cervantes' masterpiece, it is not dominant. In fact in *El Buscón* we have only an isolated example of an apparent violation serving as a textual strategy to emphasize a turning point in the novel. Galdós's "La novela en el tranvía," then, seems to project the imprint of both Cervantes and Quevedo by violating the fictional mode with the intrusion of characters from an embedded serial novel into the "real" world, a violation then negated by the logic of the narrator's temporary insanity. That only recently the presence of a metafictional mode in the works discussed has captured the attention of critics seems to corroborate the theory of reader expectations.[18] It would seem that critics did not recognize its presence in these works because they were not prepared to expect it. Yet consciously or subconsciously the novelists built on one another's strategies, and whereas the process of assimilation between Cervantes and Galdós took nearly three hundred years, with the emergence of the twentieth century that process was accelerated. The present century's preoccupation with novelistic self-commentary, therefore, is nothing more than a modern expression of strategies developed over several eras.

Chapter Two

Fiction on a Palimpsest: *Niebla*

The twentieth century in Spanish literary history was ushered in by what is popularly known as the Generation of '98. Although the date refers to the end of the nineteenth century (the Spanish American War of 1898), the novelists identified with this generation rebelled against nineteenth-century literary expression, especially against the tenets of realism. Innovation, therefore, was one of their primary concerns, and in the novel the innovations inevitably led to various forms and degrees of novelistic self-commentary.

One prominent form of novelistic self-commentary involves interior duplication, or what has been defined as "autotextualité."[1] In its most obvious manifestation this is a story-within-a-story device, with the embedded story reflecting the framing story. In Azorín's *Doña Inés* (1925), for example, a legend associated with a statue not only reflects but determines the life of the protagonists; the legend becomes their story, a type of fiction-begetting-fiction effect. Ramón Pérez de Ayala, in two novels that are actually a single work, *Tigre Juan* and *El curandero de su honra* (1926) [*Tiger Juan* and *The Healing of His Honor*] at one point divides the pages into two columns, one relating the activities of the male protagonist and the other the simultaneous activities of the female protagonist. Such a device, also a type of interior duplication but not in the same sense as *Doña Inés*, lays bare the temporal-spatial conventions fiction depends on to create the illusion of simultaneous action. In Ramón de Valle Inclán's *Tirano Banderas* (1926) [*The Tyrant Banderas*], another technique exposing temporal-spatial conventions comes into play. First of all, what turns out to be the conclusion of the story appears in the form of a prologue to the novel, followed by yet other cases in which the textual sequence of events does not correspond to the chronological order of the story. In another device that tends toward novelistic self-commentary, the protagonist and most of the other characters are described as puppets, simulacrums so contrived that any illusion that they are real people is swept aside. Yet all of the anti-realist devices noted, as well as others,[2] represent at best limited novelistic self-commentary. Miguel de Unamuno's *Niebla* (1914) [*Mist*], on the other hand, features several blatant violations of the fictional mode. In fact, many still consider *Niebla* as the Hispanic novel's most radical attack on the conventions of fiction.

The initial reception of *Niebla* suggests that reader expectations in general were not ready for Unamuno's radical modal violations. Most early critics of the novel tended to dismiss it as an anti-novel, preferring to direct their attention to Unamuno's more conventional works. In fact, only in the past decade has there been a noticeable shift in preference for *Niebla*, and an accompanying influx of analyses focused on the famous author-character-reader confrontations within the novel.[3] These analyses, which tend to offer existential explanations for the confrontations, have played an important role in shaping present-day receptions of the novel. Building from the past critical generation's readings of the novel as truth versus fiction, reality versus dream, I would like to focus now on the fictional process underlying such effects. If the past generation of critics was justifiably intrigued by *Niebla*'s illusion that fiction and reality are one and the same, the present generation is more inclined to find the textual strategies involved in creating such an illusion as intriguing as the illusion itself.

One of Unamuno's strategies for creating the illusion that reality and fiction are one is to destroy the illusion that the worlds of the fictive author and of the text-act reader can never merge with the world of the story. To effect the destruction of such an illusion (or perhaps, more accurately, to effect the illusion of the destruction of such an illusion), Unamuno unmasks the linguistic ontology of author and reader as well as that of the characters.[4] And whereas the unmasking climax occurs when the protagonist confronts the fictive author near the end of the novel, the key moments leading up to the confrontation occur in a framing device consisting of two prologues and an epilogue, and within the framed construct in a discussion of a novel one of the characters is supposedly writing.

The initial section of the frame, a prologue written by one Víctor Goti, creates an almost immediate conflict between reality and fiction when Víctor turns out to be one of the characters of the novel. What initially seemed to be a fairly common nonfictional introduction to the novel therefore suddenly becomes a part of the fictional text. As a result, the message of the opening statement of the prologue changes completely in retrospect:

> Se empeña don Miguel de Unamuno en que ponga yo un prólogo a este su libro en que relata la tan lamentable historia de mi buen amigo Augusto Pérez y su misteriosa muerte, y yo no puedo menos sino escribirlo, porque los deseos del señor Unamuno son para mí mandatos en la más genuina acepción de este vocablo.[5]

> [Don Miguel de Unamuno insists that I do the prologue for his book in which he relates the very sad story of my good friend Augusto Pérez and his mysterious death, and I have no recourse but to write it, since Mr. Unamuno's wishes are my commands in the strictest sense of the word.]

In the beginning Víctor is talking to his text reader as if both existed in the real world, and the message seems to be nothing more than a polite cliché expressing Víctor's indebtedness to Unamuno. In contrast the message to the text-act reader, once he realizes Víctor's fictionality, becomes a comical understatement of authorial omnipotence. The text-act reader must retrospectively revise his initial reading of the passage and now contemplate the implications of a fictitious character confessing that he is subservient to his creator, the real author. Moreover, even in mentioning the real author this character has violated the boundary separating their worlds.

The violation of the fictive author's world is much more blatant, however, in a subsequent passage. No sooner does the character profess his complete subservience to his author/creator than he rebels. The rebellion centers on the explanation of the death of the novel's protagonist, Augusto Pérez. After first declaring that Unamuno is mistaken in his explanation of how Augusto died, Víctor adds demurely: "pero no es cosa de que me ponga yo ahora aquí a discutir en este prólogo con mi prologado" (p. 15) ["but it is not appropriate for me to argue here in this prologue with the person whom I am prologuizing"]. The use of the term "prologado," the product of the verb "prologar," is a subtle strategy for signaling that all the characters are merely verbal constructs. Furthermore, Víctor's use of the possessive adjective "mi prologado" defines Unamuno as a product of his, Víctor's, own discoursing. The character's rebellion, as a result, goes far beyond the sense of equality implicit in his contradiction of the author's explanation of Augusto's death; Víctor, a character, is claiming credit for creating Unamuno, the author. Thus this Unamuno is subtly defined as merely another linguistic dimension of the text, a sign system emerging from another sign system labeled Víctor Goti. (Real people cannot exist within a fictional world; signs merely masquerade as people.) In short, the novel begins by attacking not only the illusion that the authorial voice constitutes the Word, but also the illusion that the world of the fictive author is an inviolable dimension of the fictional mode. This first prologue, therefore, functions as a sign pointing at the novel as pure language dependent on arbitrary conventions for all the illusions it creates.

The conventions of fiction come under further attack with a post-prologue in which Unamuno not only answers Víctor, but threatens him:

Y debe andarse mi amigo y prologuista Goti con mucho tiento en discutir así mis decisiones, porque si me fastidia mucho acabaré por hacer con él lo que con su amigo Pérez hice, y es que lo dejaré morir o le mataré a guisa de médico . . . o dejan morir al enfermo por miedo a matarle, o le matan por miedo de que se les muera. Y así, yo soy capaz de matar a Goti si veo que se me va a morir, o de dejarle morir si temo haber de matarle. [pp. 17-18]

[And my friend and prologue writer Goti better go easy in disputing in such a way my decisions, because if he irritates me too much I will end up doing with him what I did with his friend Pérez, that is to say, I will allow him to die or I will kill him the way physicians do it . . . they either allow the patient to die for fear of killing him, or kill him for fear that he will die on them. And so I am capable of killing Goti if I see that he is going to die on me, or of allowing him to die if I am afraid I will have to kill him.]

In spite of the would-be threat here, by the act of electing to answer his own character the fictive author has all but destroyed the distinction between author and character; they exist on the same narrative level and consequently the illusion of the fictive author's power over his character vanishes. And of course even the threat itself ironically underscores the fictive author's impotence. In the final analysis he can only juxtapose his own discourses with those of the character, producing an effect not unlike that of two children, or puppets, challenging one another. So the message to the text-act reader—as opposed to the fictive author's attempt to impress his text reader with his authorial power—is that the fictive author and the character alternately create and are created by one another; each is but a sign system generating and then being generated by the other. But the attack on the conventions of fiction is not complete until the text-act reader himself is also reduced to a linguistic entity.

The identification of the text-act reader as a dimension of the fictional discourse is done by means of the most subtle textual strategy of the frame, and occurs when the fictive Unamuno begins his response to Víctor: "De buena gana discutiría aquí alguna de las afirmaciones de mi prologuista, Víctor Goti, pero como estoy en el secreto de su existencia—la de Goti—, prefiero dejarle la entera responsabilidad de lo que en ese su prólogo dice" (p. 17) ["I would willingly argue here with some of the statements of my prologue writer, Víctor Goti, but since I am in on the secret of his existence—that of Goti—, I prefer to leave him with the entire responsiblity for what he says in his prologue"]. The image of the text-act reader is signaled by the parenthetical clarification, "su existencia—la de Goti." Since the possessive adjective "su" is so ambiguous—an ambiguity impossible to reflect in an English translation, for it can refer to his, her, their, or your, both singular and plural—the ostensible purpose is to clarify its ambiguity. Yet given the discursive context in which Víctor is the only apparent referent, the parenthetical clarification creates confusion rather than eliminating it. In fact, the discord of an ambiguous clarification is itself a sign pointing toward the text-act reader, the only other logical referent for the possessive "su."[6] What more subtle way to signal the text-act reader's always-present absence? But of course (and again the contradiction), once his presence has been signaled he can no longer be considered absent or merely implied. In fact, just as beyond the fictive Unamuno who speaks in the post-prologue there is the *persona* of another Unamuno determining what the verbal construct labeled Unamuno will say, so there emerges another text-act reader beyond the one that is exposed by the parenthetical statement. Metafiction's violations, in other words, merely destroy one set of illusions to replace it with another. Yet the violation of the world of the text-act reader does signal that the intended recipient of the discourses is an essential dimension of any novel's linguistic system; he is the creative force inspiring the discourses, and at the same time the product of them. Again, as in the case of the fictive author, it is a question of language rather than people, of linguistic signs responding to other linguistic signs.

The epilogue, which completes the outside frame, addresses much more directly the question of language as a conveyer of illusions. Since the epilogue is composed primarily of the discourses of Augusto's dog, Orfeo, it destroys any remaining illusion that *Niebla* is a mirror of what is generally conceived as reality. Furthermore, Orfeo himself theorizes about illusion, the illusion that man uses language to convey his true feelings, that words become one with objects and concepts, that lies are truth.

Orfeo's concern with language and illusion is inspired by his master's death. He recalls the difficulty they had communicating, and adds that dogs only really understand when humans howl because howling is the only natural sound dogs make. In fact barking, he says, is something dogs do to imitate man, who, "ladra a su manera, habla, y eso le ha servido para inventar lo que no hay y no fijarse en lo que hay. En cuanto le ha puesto un nombre a algo, ya no ve este algo, no hace sino oír el nombre que le puso, o verle escrito. La lengua le sirve para mentir, inventar lo que no hay y confundirse" (p. 164) ["barks in his own way, he talks, and that has allowed him to invent what is not there and to ignore what is there. As soon as he has placed a name on something, he no longer sees this something, he only hears the name that he placed on it, or he only sees its written signifier. Language allows him to lie, to invent what does not exist and to become confused"]. Orfeo's comments in effect summarize the essence of the novel itself: a creation designed to enable language to fulfill its natural function to invent what does not exist. And by virtue of the other half of the frame, the prologues, the focus switches from the invented product to the process of inventing. By laying bare the conventions that make fiction seem real, the frame assures that what is really there, language and its incredible creative capacity, will not be ignored.

The frame is a sign, therefore, pointing simultaneously at itself and at the construct it encloses.

In pointing at itself, the frame calls attention to its purely linguistic quintessence; in pointing at the anecdote centered on Augusto's unsuccessful courtship of the beautiful Eugenia, it imparts to this anecdote a tinge of pure fabulation. It is the case of one sign (the prologues and epilogue) being superimposed on another sign (the framed construct).[7] The story cannot be separated in the reading process from the metafictional effects of the strategies employed in the frame surrounding it.

The imprint of the frame on the anecdote is discernible from the moment Augusto first sees Eugenia and follows her until she disappears into her house. Standing alone in the street he discovers that her physical absence is no major obstacle to his vision of her: "Estuvo así sugiriéndose la figura de Eugenia, y como apenas si la había visto, tuvo que figurársela. Merced a esta labor de evocación fue surgiendo a su fantasía una figura vagarosa ceñida de ensueños" (p. 31) ["He remained that way a while trying to make himself create Eugenia's appearance, and since he had barely seen her, he was forced to imagine it. Thanks to this evocative effort, an image vaguely tinted by daydreams began to emerge in his fantasy"]. A character of the story has just created another character through imagination and language. Furthermore, as creator he immediately declares his authority over his creation: "Mi Eugenia, sí, la mía—iba diciéndose—, esta que me estoy forjando a solas, y no la otra, no la de carne y hueso . . . !" (p. 31) ["My Eugenia, yes, mine—he was saying to himself—, this one that I am creating by myself, and not the other one, not the one of flesh and blood . . . !"] By virtue of the imprint of the prologues, the message of the text-act reader is different from that which Augusto directs to his text reader. Augusto, naturally not aware of the frame in which he is enclosed, contrasts his imaginative creation with the "real" Eugenia ("la de carne y hueso"). His claim of ownership, then, is both true and ridiculous since he concedes that the real object of his affections is the other Eugenia. For the text-act reader, however, the supposed Eugenia of flesh and blood is no less a fantasy than the one Augusto invents; one is the fictive author's verbal construct while the other is Augusto's. Since, however, the fictive author has already been exposed in the prologue as a mere verbal construct himself, the two Eugenias are equally inventions, mere fictions.

There is also a distinct echo from the prologues when Augusto, in contrast to his earlier claim of authority over Eugenia, suddenly begins to question who is the creator and who is the creation: "¿De dónde ha brotado Eugenia? ¿Es ella una creación mía o soy creación suya yo? ¿O somos los dos creaciones mutuas, ella de mí, yo de ella? ¿No es acaso todo creación de cada cosa y cada cosa creación de todo? Y ¿qué es creación? (p. 50) ["Where has Eugenia emerged from? Is she a creation of mine, or am I a creation of hers? Or are we two mutual creations, she of me and I of her? Isn't perhaps everything the creation of everything else? And what is creation?"] Just as Víctor and the fictive Unamuno of the prologues are two sign systems giving birth to and then being born of the other, so Augusto now sees himself and Eugenia as both creator and creation of the other. And whereas on the anecdotal level Augusto's questioning concerns love and its effect on two people, for the text-act reader the issue is again language and its ability to give birth to itself. In fact all of these passages point both back at the prologues and ahead to the concluding chapters; they evoke the image of the conflict between Víctor and the fictive Unamuno in the opening frames, and they augur Augusto's ultimate direct confrontation with the fictive Unamuno near the end of the novel. In short, they contribute to the process of switching the focus from the illusions to the creation of the illusions.[8] Such a process is crystallized within the framed construct when Víctor, also a novelist, begins a discussion with Augusto about the novel he is writing. This discussion marks the point where the novel turns definitively inward on itself.

As the discussion begins, Víctor notes that he is writing his novel in dialogue, the purpose of which he explains: "Y sobre todo que parezca que el autor no dice las cosas por sí, no nos molesta con su personalidad, con su yo satánico. Aunque, por supuesto, todo lo que digan mis personajes lo digo yo" (p. 92) ["And above all it must appear that the author does not say things on his own account, that he does not bother us with his personality, with his satanic 'I.' Although, of course, everything that my characters say I am actually saying"]. Augusto, reacting to this claim of omnipotence, decides to challenge his novelist friend: "Sí, que empezarás creyendo que los llevas tú, de tu mano, y es fácil que acabes convenciéndote de que son ellos los que te llevan. Es muy frecuente que un autor acabe por ser juguete de sus ficciones" (p. 92) ["Yes, you will begin by believing that you are leading them by your hand, but it is likely that you will end up convincing yourself that they are the ones leading you. Very often an author ends up as the plaything of his fictions"]. The Unamuno-Víctor conflict of the prologues is now being reenacted between Víctor and Augusto. And when Augusto has the effrontery to ask what Víctor does about dialogue when only one character is present, Víctor insidiously explains: "Entonces . . . un monólogo. Y para que parezca algo así como un diálogo, invento un perro a quien el personaje se dirige" (p. 93) ["Then . . . a monologue. And in order that it may resemble somewhat a dialogue, I invent a dog to whom the character addresses himself"]. Poor Augusto, who constantly confesses his doubts and troubles to his dog Orfeo—his dramatized text addressee—has had his own fictionality thrown in his face. And even though Víctor, in a moment of exasperation, earlier challenged Augusto's claim to reality—"Y si me apuras mucho te digo que tú mismo no eres sino una pura idea, un ente de ficción" (p. 62) ["And if you press me too much I will tell you that you yourself are only a pure idea, a fictional being"]—on that occasion it was possible to lend a metaphorical interpretation to the words. Now, however, Augusto cannot ignore the fusion of his own reality with Víctor's invention. The game of fiction reigns supreme. Víctor is challenging the creative authority of the fictive author by claiming credit for the invention of his interlocutor, and even of the story of which both and his interlocutor were a part.

The text at this point becomes a palimpsest with the imprint of the prologues clearly visible behind Víctor's and Augusto's debate. By virtue, therefore, of the palimpsest's dual images we have an even more dramatic assault on the boundaries separating the world *from* which one speaks and the world *of* which one speaks, and, with the collapse of this boundary, an even more dramatic assault on the illusion that some verbal constructs are endowed with exclusively creative power while others are exclusively their products. Authors and characters, since they are merely sign systems, alternately create and are created by one another. And, of course, this creative process is all for the benefit of a text-act reader, the third creator/creation paradox constituting the fictional mode.

Again the narrative seems to be written on a palimpsest when the fictive author interrupts the discussion of Víctor's novel to appeal directly this time to the text-act reader: "Mientras Augusto y Víctor sostenían esta conversación nivolesca, yo, el autor de esta nivola, que tienes, lector, en la mano, y estás leyendo, me sonreía enigmáticamente al ver que mis nivolescos personajes estaban abogando por mí y justificando mis procedimientos" (p. 130) ["While Augusto and Víctor were sustaining this 'nivolesca' conversation, I the author of this 'nivola' that you have, reader, in your hands, and are reading, smiled enigmatically to myself upon seeing that my 'nivolescos' personages were arguing my case for me and justifying my procedures"]. While the fictive author apparently commits this transgression of narrative level in an attempt to affirm his hierarchical superiority over his characters, his direct appeal to the text-act reader indicates his awareness that someone else will pass judgment on his claim, a someone else who literally holds in his hands the fate of him and the characters. Yet at the same time that the fictive Unamuno seems to concede omnipotence to his reader, he may have something else in mind. The fictive author's enigmatic smile, although ostensibly inspired by Víctor's and Augusto's conversation, could also be directed at the text-act reader as a signal of the sinister trick he, the author, has just played on his interlocutor. By addressing him directly, he has dramatized the reader's linguistic ontology; he has made him an explicit dimension of the text. When the fictive author destroys in this way the illusion that readers exist only in the real world, he paves the way for creating a new illusion, the illusion that we real readers are in fact fictitious.

The architect of the new illusion is not the fictive Unamuno but Víctor, whose answer to Unamuno's intrusion is an explanation to Augusto of the need for a new suspension of disbelief:

Y además, que si, como te decía, un nivolista oculto que nos está oyendo toma nota de nuestras palabras para reproducirlas un día, el lector de la nivola llega a dudar, siquiera fuese un fugitivo momento, de su propia realidad de bulto y se crea a su vez no más que un personaje nivolesco, como nosotros. [p. 146]

[And besides, just in case, as I was telling you, a hidden "nivolista" is listening to us and taking notes of our words so as to reproduce them someday, the reader of the "nivola" may come to doubt, if only for a fleeting moment, his own concrete reality and to consider himself as nothing more than a "nivolesco" character, just as we are.]

The one convention left intact after so many violations is that which encourages the real reader to identify consciously or subconsciously with the text-act reader. As a result, our instinct to identify places us now squarely within the text. The textual strategy of destroying the illusion of the text-reader's separation from the text creates the new illusion of the real reader's physical involvement in it.

For many, the process of destroying fiction's conventions and illusions is centered on, if not limited to, the final three chapters of *Niebla*. In them the direct confrontation occurs between Augusto and the fictive Unamuno. Although these chapters are undeniably the most spectacular displays of violations and consequently have received by far the most critical attention, if not anticlimatic they are at least dependent on the process of fusing into a single sign, by means of Víctor's novel, the frame and the framed construct.

As the past critical generation so perceptively noted, *Niebla* makes us feel that truth and fiction, reality and dream, are indeed one and the same. In fact, at the end of Unamuno's last novel, *San Manuel Bueno, mártir* (1931) [*Saint Manuel Good, Martyr*], the fictive author violates the world of the first-person narrator to argue the same basic thesis:

¿Que se parece mucho a otras cosas que yo he escrito? Esto nada prueba contra su objetividad, su originalidad. ¿Y sé yo, además, si no he creado fuera de mí seres reales y efectivos, de alma inmortalidad? ¿Sé yo si aquel Augusto Pérez, el de mi novela *Niebla*, no tenía razón al pretender ser más real, más objetivo que yo mismo, que pretendía haberlo inventado? De la realidad de este San Manuel Bueno, mártir, tal como me le ha revelado su discípula e hija espiritual Angela Carballino, de esta realidad no se me ocurre dudar. Creo en ella más que creía el mismo santo; creo en ella más que creo en mi propia realidad. [p. 82]

[So it resembles other things I have written? This doesn't prove anything against its objectivity, its originality. And anyway, do I know if perhaps I have created real and authentic beings, with immortal souls? Do I know if that Augusto Pérez, the one from my novel *Niebla*, wasn't right upon claiming to be more real and objective than I, the very one who thought he had created him? About San Manuel Bueno, the martyr's, reality, just as his disciple and spiritual daughter Angela Carballino has revealed it to me, about this reality I have no reason to doubt. I believe in it more than the saint himself believed in it, more than I believe in my own reality.]

The textual strategy behind the theme of fiction versus reality in the case of *Niebla* involves foregrounding the fascinating capacity of language to give birth to itself, to create illusion in the very act of destroying illusion. Another reading of the title itself, therefore, is that Unamuno is inviting us to look through the mist created by the artifices of fiction to the process of invention underlying the artifices. Thus the laying bare of conventions and artifices by works such as *Niebla* and *San Manuel Bueno, mártir* does not denigrate the work of fiction but rather glorifies its inventive capacity. And whether Unamuno would admit or would even be aware of the imprint of Cervantes, Quevedo, Galdós, and perhaps others on his strategies is a moot question. At some level he assimilated their models of tentative or pseudo-violations and carried them to an extreme: fictive authors, characters, and text-act reader united into a single world where apparently nothing exists but the dream of existence. Such is the disturbing yet fascinating illusion Unamuno offers us by means of his flagrant violations of the fictional mode.

Chapter Three

Codes versus Modes: *Locura y muerte de nadie* and *La novia del viento*

Notwithstanding the example of *Niebla* and of some other novels mentioned at the beginning of the previous chapter, the metafictional mode is not predominant in the Generation of '98. Indeed, before critics became obsessed with metafiction, *Niebla* was read primarily for its existential content. As suggested in the previous chapter, the self-commentary of the novels of the Generation of '98 can be seen primarily as anti-realist techniques. That is to say, by eschewing the illusion that they are about real people involved in real events, the novels of the Generation of '98 foreground their own literariness; they indirectly comment on themselves by making novelistic art itself one of their implicit concerns. Yet often overshadowing the implicit problem of art in these novels is the implicit problem of the nation and the Spaniard—not so much in the sociopolitical as in the ontological sense. The subsequent literary movement in Spain, on the other hand, brings the problem of art to the forefront and relegates to the background existential and social concerns. I am referring, of course, to the vanguardist movement of the 1920s and 1930s with its resurrected motto, "art for art's sake."[1] Such a movement, therefore, and specifically the work of its leading novelist, Benjamín Jarnés, is a logical focal point to explore in more detail the problematic relationship between experimentation-artfulness and metafiction.

Jarnés was not only the leading vanguardist novelist but, as a contributor to the *Revista de Occidente*, one of the foremost spokesmen for its artistic tenets. Perhaps influenced by his reputation as a spokesman for the movement, critics tend to define his novels as theoretical essays or experiments, often citing a lyrical, subjective style as the device through which Jarnés reduces all his novels to treatises on art.[2] Although there is a certain justification in such a claim, it fails to distinguish between his use of elaborate artfulness as one type of novelistic self-commentary, and the adaptation he makes of the Cervantes, Quevedo, Galdós, and Unamuno models for exposing the narrative process itself. Thus it is a case, on the one hand of foregrounding literary codes, and on the other of violating the modes or laws of fiction. To demonstrate the distinction I am proposing, I have selected *Locura y muerte de nadie* (1929) [*The Insanity and Death of Nobody*] as an example of self-commentary through codes, and *La novia del viento* (1940) [*The Wind's Bride*] as an example of a violation of the modes of fiction.

Anecdotally, *Locura y muerte de nadie* concerns the efforts of the protagonist, Juan Sánchez, to gain recognition as something other than just another face in the mass of humanity. Yet from the very beginning of the novel, where his signature is challenged in a bank, to the end, when he falls victim to a speeding truck, society refuses to recognize his individuality, as his death is likened to the mere erasure of his signature. In fact, Juan is such a nonentity that it is probably not accurate to refer to him as the protagonist of the novel. The source of focalization is Arturo, Juan's friend, who is unknowingly drawn into a love triangle involving Juan's wife and his business partner. Arturo serves as ironic observer of the wife's and business partner's machinations and of Juan's futile struggle against anonymity, a struggle culminating with a failed suicide attempt immediately before his accidental death under the wheels of the truck.

As one might suspect from even this schematic outline of the story, the novel is generally read as an expression of two of Ortega y Gasset's basic concerns: the threat of a dehumanized mass society and the need to "dehumanize" art so as to reflect that threat.[3] A more recent reading, however, views the work as a metafiction whose metaphors function as indices of fictionality rather than of dehumanization.[4] Whereas the author of the latter thesis limits the novel to its metafictional dimension, I will be arguing that the theme of dehumanization and fictional self-commentary are inseparable. Furthermore, the strategy for self-commentary in Jarnés's novel contrasts with those strategies examined so far in this study.

By using parody to emphasize the codes or formal constraints distinguishing other literary genres and styles, *Locura y muerte de nadie* foregrounds its own code system.[5] In short, the novel is about its own novelistic style and at the same time about the society such a style reflects.

The use of parody as a device for foregrounding literary codes or formal constraints is most striking in chapters four and five. These chapters present Arturo arriving at Juan's home following an afternoon of lovemaking with a woman he knows only by the name Rebeca. Juan, whom Arturo met earlier at the bank, shows him a nude painting and Arturo recognizes the model, even though her face is covered, as Rebeca. At that point Rebeca enters the room with a man, and Juan introduces them as his wife Matilde and his cousin and business partner, Alfredo. Arturo is shocked not only by the discovery that his lover is his new friend's wife, but also by the memory that Alfredo is the name Matilde uttered that afternoon in a fit of passion during their lovemaking. As the four then sit down at the table for dinner, the narrator remarks: "Del conflicto dramático—porque estamos en presencia de un profundo conflicto dramático—a Arturo sólo le preocupa, en primer término, para no precipitar el desenlace, recordar bien el verdadero nombre de Rebeca"[6] ["The only thing that bothers Arturo about the dramatic conflict—because we are witnessing a profound dramatic conflict—is above all to remember the true name of Rebeca so as not to precipitate the denouement"]. The parenthetical repetition of the term "dramatic conflict" diminishes rather than increases the tragic potential of this situation. And although such a gratuitous interpretation calls attention to the presence of the narrator, it is not the same type of violation of a fictional mode examined up to this point—the type, for example, where a narrator addresses the characters themselves.[7] In fact, rather than a true violation of narrative worlds, this kind of aside, generally labeled an intrusive or editorial comment, is all too typical of a certain novelistic style prevalent in the nineteenth century. That is, the aside is coded and therefore draws even more attention to the conventionality of the romantic intrigue inspiring it. Such conventionality, furthermore, collides with the very concept of "art for art's sake," a collision that foregrounds literary style itself.[8] In short, the emphasis has switched from the hermeneutic code—what will happen—to the literary codes distinguishing certain types of plot situations.

Although the narrator initiates the process of foregrounding literary code systems, he quickly shifts that function to Arturo. The shift is effected by changing the object of focalization from an outside view of the four characters seated at the dinner table to the inner thoughts of each one. When the focus falls on Arturo, he expresses himself with a vocabulary tinted by critical terminology: "El azar nunca fue tan caprichoso conmigo. En una misma tarde me encuentro con tres personajes representativos, muy dignos de estudio, probablemente víctimas de otras tantas enfermedades incurables; peligrosos, eso sí, para un puro contemplador que se decide perder su pureza, a mezclarse en su drama" (p. 1434) ["Chance was never so capricious with me. On the same afternoon I find myself with three representative personages very worthy of study, probably victims of numerous other incurable diseases; dangerous, yes, for a pure observer who decides to lose his purity and become a part of their drama"]. The reference to himself as a "pure" observer about to lose his purity conveys a tone of self-mockery as his contemplative self separates from his physical self. In fact, he creates the sensation of a literary critic commenting on a dramatic work in which he has decided to play a role. As the scene unfolds, his dual role of critical observer and participant becomes even more clearly defined:

Y esta misma ausencia de elementos concretos le empuja a mirar a sus compañeros de mesa como elementos obstractos de un drama latente, de un juego cuyas cartas nadie se atreve a arrojar sobre la mesa. El, que por complacer a la fracasada Rebeca, está leyendo estos días un lote copioso de novelas del siglo XIX, define con esta vaga fórmula la extraña situación íntima del grupo: "Sobre nosotros se cierne la tragedia". [p. 1436]

[And this same absence of concrete elements inspires him to look at his table companions as abstract elements of a potential drama, of a game in which no one dares to throw his cards on the table. He, who wishing to please the unfortunate Rebeca, is reading at present a whole collection of nineteenth-century novels, defines the strange intimate situation of the group with this vague formula: "Tragedy is hanging over us".]

Tragedy, when reduced to formulaic terms, becomes a purely literary conceit. Since, furthermore, the source of the conceit is identified as a certain sentimental novelistic genre of the past century, it is really a question of hackneyed melodrama. Again there is a clash between such a genre and the well-publicized tenets of the vanguardist movement. This type of parody, by calling attention to the question of plot conventions, constitutes a certain kind of novelistic self-commentary. And whereas in the previous example such self-commentary was orchestrated by the narrator, now, even though the voice is still that of the narrator, the viewing position is Arturo's consciousness.[9] This consciousness, detached from his physical being, draws on literary conventionality to describe the bizarre scene, a scene of which he is a critical observer and, at the same time, in which he is a participating actor.

Arturo's role as critic, however, soon eclipses that of actor as he considers the implications of four participants in the potential tragedy:

> Una ligera meditación acerca del número cuatro comienza a tranquilizarle sobre el posible final . . . la tragedia comienza asimismo a reducirse de tamaño, al crecer el número de actores esenciales. Cuatro, principian a ser excesivos. Comienza a intervenir el elemento irónico. Tres, mantiene la escena, y uno, contempla: y todo el que verdaderamente contempla, termina por desgajarse de lo contemplado. [pp. 1436-37]

> [A slight consideration of the number four begins to calm him about the possible final scene . . . the tragedy also begins to become reduced in size as the number of essential actors increases. Four begin to become excessive. The ironic element begins to intervene. Three dominate the scene, and one observes: and everyone who really contemplates, ends up by separating himself from that which he is contemplating.]

By virtue of his critical detachment, he has recognized that the scene in which he is physically involved does not conform to the code system; the structural components of his situation do not correspond to those of the genre Tragedy. Literary conventionality saves him. *Locura y muerte de nadie,* therefore, is not really about the story of Juan, Matilde, Alfredo, and Arturo; it is about stories in general, and about itself in relation to the conventions of storytelling. So the foregrounding of a code system from another era functions self-referentially to point at this novel and its particular code system. The foregrounded codes, in turn, also function referentially as they point toward a society mired in its own conventionality, in its own dehumanizing forces. In short, the codes of

Locura y muerte de nadie are both literary and social; they point at both the novel itself and the social context in which it was created.

Jarnés's novel has justifiably been identified with the vanguardist movement in Spain. As the preceding analysis suggests, literary borrowing in the form of parody is an important dimension of such a movement. But the borrowing does not involve merely inserting one passage into another. Gustavo Pérez Firmat has demonstrated that the incorporation of a passage from one text into another transforms both the borrowed and the incorporating text into a new text.[10] The formal constraints of the borrowed text are broken merely by transposing it to another context; the formal constraints of the incorporating text are also broken by the infusion into it of alien literary codes. After reading a novel like *Locura y muerte de nadie,* it is doubtful that one would ever react to post-vanguardist melodrama again without seeing in it the traces from a parodied version. The textual strategy of foregrounding literary codes in this novel represents a type of novelistic self-commentary and a break from melodramatic novelistic styles. It does not, however, represent a breaking of the laws of narrative discourse themselves.[11] Jarnés engaged in that more radical self-commentary in *La novia del viento.*

The first section of *La novia del viento* is dated 1926 and initially appeared as a short story in *La Gaceta Literaria,* entitled "Andromeda." The middle and final sections, dated 1939, were added to form the novel as it was published in 1940. Sections one and three resemble *Locura y muerte de nadie,* since in them literary codes are foregrounded as a means of parodying conventionality. In the middle section, however, Jarnés adopts the more radical technique of violating narrative modes and in so doing exposes the arbitrary conventions constraining narrative fiction itself.

The ancedote of the first section concerns the discovery by Julio of a nude woman, the victim of highway robbers, tied to an olive tree. Since the crime occurred in woods outside the city, Julio returns to the casino to borrow a car. It is dawn by the time he can return with the car, pick up the victim, and take her back to the city. Her modesty protected only by a blanket, they drive around the city until the shops open and Julio can buy her clothing. Once she has dressed and applied makeup, Julio recognizes her as a cabaret dancer whose pinup picture he carries in his wallet. Although she invites him to visit her at the hotel where she lives or at the club where she dances, the narrator ends the section by explaining that Julio felt he had fulfilled his role as hero and was not sufficiently motivated to see the adventure through to another stage. In the third section (the second section has been called an essay on the novel[12]), Julio becomes involved, however, in another adventure. At a dance he meets Brunilda and her father, accepts their invitation to accompany them on a hike up a hill named "La novia del viento," and on their return shows Brunilda the tree where he rescued the dancer Carmela. When he later receives a letter from Carmela asking him to come to visit her in another city where she is now working, Brunilda goes into action. She invites him to her studio where she unveils a painting displaying herself nude and tied to the same tree where Julio discovered Carmela. Julio, first seduced by the provocative pictorial representation, is apparently physically seduced by Brunilda. Brunilda then ensures that the plastic image that finally aroused him will not serve as a rival in the future when she destroys the painting at the novel's end.

Brunilda's destruction of the painting is a logical response to Julio's tendency to find his sensual gratification in plastic images and therefore to prefer adornment to naked reality. For example, after discovering Carmela nude and spending the night with her as she is imperfectly covered by only a blanket, once she has finished dressing and applying makeup, Julio confesses: "Para mí, comenzó usted a existir ahora. —¿Vestida? —Sí, Carmela"[13] ["As far as I am concerned, you began to exist just now. —With my clothes on? —Yes, Carmela"]. The woman who has just come into existence corresponds, of course, to the picture he carries in his wallet.

In addition to his attraction to plastic images, Julio depends on literary models to explain his own experiences, a dependence the fictive author mockingly reinforces with the titles of the three sections and of several of the chapters ("Andromeda," "Epimetheus' Digression," "Brunilda in Flames," "The Birth of the Hero," "Transfiguration," "The Return of Perseus," and "Death of the Dragon"). These titles serve as parodic devices within the context of Julio's adventures, and mock his penchant for considering art as a substitute for, rather than an enrichment of, reality.

Julio's propensity for confusing art and reality—perhaps intended as a commentary on realistic art in general—is ridiculously evident when he first discovers the naked Carmela tied to a tree: "A Julio no le sorprendió verla completamente desnuda. Siempre la había visto así en los cuadros del Museo y en el tomo quinto de la Enciclopedia Espasa" (p. 16) ["It did not surprise Julio to see her completely naked. He had always seen her that way in the paintings of the museum in the fifth volume of the *Encyclopedia Espasa*"]. This reference to Rubens's "Enchained Andromeda," a reference clarified on the next page,[14] not only mocks Julio as he dismisses with a scholarly footnote the prurient potential of the situation, but comically signals the victim's physical proportions. Julio, nevertheless, is oblivious to the captive's feminine endowments as he casts himself into the mythic role: "—¿Dónde está el dragón? — ¿Qué dragón? —Perdone. Era un tropo" (p. 18) ["—Where's the dragon? —What dragon? —Excuse me. That was merely a trope"]. Much like Arturo in *Locura y muerte de nadie*, Julio is aware of his involvement in literary conventionality. Such an awareness is most evident as he observes Carmela (or Star as he has opted to call her) put on the clothes purchased when the shops open:

Al ceñirse Star la faja, Julio recordó a los pintores realistas del ochocientos, obligados a fabricarse una realidad antes de pintarla. Solía rectificar en los modelos el talle, deformado por el corsé, como el paisajista coloca un buey en medio del prado para corregir una elipsis de armonía, o añade a los ojos de los recién nacidos de Belén una luz espiritual de mozo de quince años, para ser dócil al dogma. [p. 55]

[As Star fastened the sash around her waist, Julio remembered the eighteenth-century realist painters who were forced to fabricate a reality before they could paint it. They used to adjust the waistline of their models, deformed by corsets, just as the landscapist places an ox in the middle of a meadow so as to correct a lack of harmony, or adds a spiritual light of a fifteen year old to the eyes of newborn babies in Bethlehem, just to be more faithful to the dogma.]

Unlike Arturo of the earlier novel, however, Julio is incapable of assuming a critical view and distancing himself from literary conventionality for more than a moment. In fact, he has reduced art to a rote; rather than a stimulus to his senses and imagination, it provides him with set patterns of behavior enabling him to escape a confrontation with reality.

In addition to providing Julio with models for his own conduct, the literary references of the first and third sections allow the text-act reader to recognize the ironic relationships between Julio's trials and those of the mythic heroes of the models. Indeed, the fictive author seems especially concerned with guiding the reading process of the text-act reader, as evidenced by the following passage after one of Julio's philosophical treatises: "Hasta aquí llegan aquella noche las reflexiones de Julio, reflexiones escritas para lectores graves, enemigos de todo humorismo" (p. 72) ["Julio's ruminations that night ended at this point, ruminations written for serious readers, enemies of any type of humor"]. A somber and humorless reader clearly is not the intended recipient of the juxtapositions of Julio on the one hand and the mythic heroes on the other. In fact, by defining in explicit terms Julio's implied text addressee, the fictive author underscores the distinction between such an embedded addressee and the text-act reader stationed outside the boundaries of the story.

The concept itself of the text-act reader is further explored in the middle section, where the strategy for the novelistic self-commentary involves a violation of fictional modes. In effect, the middle section functions as a reading of the first section. Added some ten years after the creation of part one, it offers a plot summary of the latter that seems designed to recall the action for the initial addressee. In addition, it summarizes reader reactions to the first part and offers advice on how to read the third section. In short, this middle section represents a response by the fictive author to his own story and to the reading of that story by others. He is his own reader, and as such he is violating the world of the original text-act reader to whom the implied message concerns the act of reading and misreading as it relates to *La novia del viento*.

The fictive author begins his self-reading by citing those who decoded the message as he intended it:

Así fue escrita. Así fue—por muchos—placenteramente leída. Sobre todo por algunos expertos, ya cansados de leer esas historias pasionales que se detienen golosamente en el punto y hora en que el héroe acaba de desnudar al objeto amado. ¡Con qué vehemencia elogiaban esta nueva modalidad en desenlaces novelescos! —Es admirable—decían—ese modo de no dar fin a una novela. El epílogo queda a cargo del lector. El lector colabora imaginando epílogos. [p. 67]

[That's the way it was written. And that's the way it was enjoyably read—by many. Above all by some experts, by those tired of reading those passionate stories that linger over the moment in which the hero has just undressed the object of his affection. How vehemently they praised this new mode in novelistic denouement! —It's admirable—they said—that method of not ending a novel. The epilogue is left in the hands of the reader. The reader collaborates by imagining his own epilogues.]

These supposedly real readers successfully projected themselves into the role of the original text-act reader, and by citing their receptions the fictive author is signaling to his new text-act reader how the work should be received. In short, he is defining appropriate past reader receptions to shape future reader expectations for the expanded version of his novel: "Pero los mitos—como verá el que leyere—se encadenan inexorablemente" (p. 65) ["But myths—as he who reads on will see—become inexorably linked to one another"].

The need to prepare reader expectations is glaringly evident when the fictive author explains how less sophisticated readers received the original shortened version of his novel:

Pero nunca falta el discrepante que—decepcionado—pregunta por las zonas reales de la aventura, por los orígenes del suceso, por la hoja clínica de los héroes . . . Queda incomprendido el héroe. Julio, mozuelo caído de las nubes, personaje fabuloso, inconcreto. Hijo del capricho, no de un estudio severo de la humanidad. [pp. 67-68]

[But there is always the exception who—disappointed—wants to know about the true-life elements of the adventure, about the origins of the event, about the clinical case history of the heroes. . . . The hero is never understood, Julio, a young guy who just drops out of the sky, a fantasy character, amorphous. A child of whim rather than the product of a careful empirical study of human nature.]

Such a reading, of course, reflects someone conditioned to realist expositions, devoid of imagination and intolerant of any departure from cause-and-effect novelistic principles. In a word, such a person is guilty of misreading by insisting on a literal reading of the characters and events.

In addition to the problem of reader expectations by those accustomed to a more literal level of reading, the fictive author

Codes versus Modes 55

must account for receptions distorted by overreading. To that end he quotes a supposed letter from a morally indignant reader who complains:

Y parece mentira que un hombre a quien suponíamos tan cabal se haya complacido en pasear de tal modo a una lozana mujer, a juzgar por la pintura, después de abandonarla desnuda, quién sabe cuánto tiempo, a merced de las más lúbricas miradas. Ese paseo, a solas, por una carretera, toda una noche, provocando con sus malignas reticencias la sensualidad de muchos jóvenes incautos que seducidos por la novedad. . . . Porque lo peor del relato no es lo que se cuenta, sino lo que se insinúa. [p. 69]

[And it seems incredible that a man we considered so prudent would allow himself to drive around in such a manner with a very well developed woman, to judge by the painting, after having abandoned her naked, God only knows how long, to the mercy of the most lascivious glances. That drive, all alone, along a highway all night long, provoking with their pernicious reticence the sensuality of many inexperienced young men who felt seduced by the novelty of it all. . . . Because the worst part of the story is not what is narrated, but what is insinuated.]

The expanded version, therefore, is a response both to a literal reading and above all to the above reading apparently inspired by malicious intent:

Y también es preciso complacer al lector zoilesco. Por eso, en algunas nuevas páginas, se intenta aquí explicar el pretérito y el futuro de Carmela y el de Julio. Con alguna alusión a la tercera figura mítica y real, al del Dragón. Las páginas que siguen pretenderán calmar las ansias de verdad histórica que suelen acometer al buen lector—y censor de novelas. [p. 69]

[And it is also necessary to placate the malicious reader. Therefore, in some new pages the past and future of Carmela and Julio will be explained. With an allusion to the third mythical and real figure, the Dragon. The following pages will attempt to calm the anxieties for historical truth that normally bother the good old reader—and censor of novels.]

Since the fictive author has gone to great pains to demonstrate that this "buen lector—y censor de novelas" is guilty of blatant misreadings, the claim that the expanded version is designed to calm such a reader's anxieties seems to project a dual message. This "buen lector" is now an embedded text reader who has been characterized not only by the letter but by the adjective "zoilesco."

Such a characterization suggests that the message to the text-act reader is the polar opposite. Rather than calming the anxieties of those looking for historical truth, the text-act reader is being signaled to look for poetic truth. Above all, he should set aside the prejudices conditioned by realist techniques and open his expectations to accommodate new forms of the novel. Thus the fictive author has violated the world of the text-act reader so as to reshape reader expectations.

The concept of new reader expectations also points to the multiple levels of reading inherent in any text, and to the need for constant rereadings. Such a rereading is precisely what the fictive author then offers in the third section entitled "Brunilda en llamas." Yet in violent conflict with the role of the mythic hero, Julio defines his completely pedestrian aspirations: "algún día, buscar la mujer dócil, sumisa, individuo más débil, que no aspira a llegar a la plena región de las ideas, ni siquiera en los actos decisivos de la vida" (p. 78) ["some day look for the docile, submissive woman, the weakest individual who does not aspire to the lofty regions of ideas, not even in the decisive acts of life"]. A new reading is suggested by this modern-day Brunilda who, by seducing him, draws Julio out of his all-too-familiar Spanish male attitude and his infatuation with plastic images and surface textures. She not only saves herself from the ring of fire perhaps symbolic of the status of Spanish women in general, but saves Julio as well. Whereas in the first part Julio forsook the nude Carmela for the pinup picture of her he carried in his billfold, in his third section Brunilda herself destroys the icon that initially aroused him. Brunilda saves Siegried in this rereading of the ancient myth, which of course is also a rereading of the first section of *La novia del viento*.

It is tempting and perhaps justified to conclude that the novelistic self-commentary of the vanguardist movement was best served by foregrounding literary codes. The primary preoccupation of novelists such as Gómez de la Serna, and Pedro Salinas in his short fiction, like that of Jarnés, is breaking from stylistic constraints rather than breaking the laws of fiction.[15] Even when Jarnés violates the modes of fiction in *La novia del viento*, the message of a need to change reader expectations on the stylistic level tends to overshadow the message concerning the laws themselves of fiction. The same basic stylistic message comes across even more clearly in *Locura y muerte de nadie* by the foregrounding of the code system. At any rate the two novels demonstrate two distinct textual strategies for novelistic self-commentary, and perhaps help clarify the distinction Alter proposes between what he calls "an elaborately artful novel" and a truly self-conscious novel.[16] It seems reasonable to conclude that for Alter, a self-conscious novel means one that violates the modes of fiction.[17]

Chapter Four

Rebellion against Models: *Don Juan* and *Orestes*

The so-called "art for art's sake" movement of the 1920s and 1930s came to an abrupt end with the Spanish Civil War (1936-1939). Although it would be an exaggeration to say that novelistic activity ceased completely during the war years,[1] most of the works emerging from that period are significant for historical rather than artistic reasons. Camilo José Cela's *La familia de Pascual Duarte* [*The Family of Pascual Duarte* in the English version], published in 1942 and soon followed by other novels displaying similar techniques, was the first of a new group whose artistic merits enabled them to transcend their historical moment.

The novelistic movement initiated by Cela's *Pascual Duarte* extended until 1962, and although a plethora of labels have been applied to it, neorealism is perhaps the most widely used and accurate.[2] Such a term, however, should not lead one to assume that these novels merely document reality. Indeed, many of the neorealistic novels are noteworthy for their complex structures and lyrical descriptions, e.g., Carmen Laforet's *Nada* (1944) [*Nothing*], Miguel Delibes' *El camino* (1950) [*The Road*], Cela's *La colmena* (1951) [*The Hive* in the English version], Ana María Matute's *Fiesta al noroeste* (1953) [*Northeast Festival*], and Rafael Sánchez Ferlosio's *El Jarama* (1956) [*The One Day of the Week* in the English version], to cite some of the more notable examples. The novels grouped under the rubric neorealism, however, display very little penchant toward experimentation with narrative modes. Prevailing wisdom suggests that the metafictional mode is incompatible with expressions of realism.[3] Notwithstanding the temptation of such an easy explanation for the hiatus of metafiction in the 1940s and 1950s, the explanation seems less than satisfactory in view of Galdós's metafictional experiments combined with the realist mode of the previous century.[4]

For all practical purposes the end of the neorealistic movement can be pinpointed to 1962, the year Luis Martín-Santos published his novel *Tiempo de silencio [Silent Time]*. Martín-Santos's novel and its successors are generally designated as the Spanish New Novel, and although that term really never has been defined adequately,[5] without question the movement marks a resurgence of narrative experimentation. By far the principal expression of such novelistic experiments takes the form of self-referential language. As opposed to what may be characterized as the transparent language of neorealism, the language of the New Novel tends to be more opaque; rather than looking through the language to the object represented, in the New Novel one tends to look more at the language itself.[6] Another less prominent type of experimentation, equally anti-neorealist, involves the use of fantasy in the form of resurrected literary or mythical models. The use of such models is similar to the type of coding Jarnés and the vanguardists accomplish with parodies. Yet unlike the vanguardists, the creators of the New Novel show a major concern with the process itself of literary borrowing. Fiction representative of this new group explores from various perspectives the concept of the work within the work, of literature as a response to literature. Such novels are more concerned with challenging and thereby updating classical literary models than with merely parodying trite novelistic styles and themes. Within the general category New Novel, the strategy of transforming classical models qualifies as the most obvious expression of novelistic self-commentary.

The first notable example of a 1960s novel transforming a classical model is Gonzalo Torrente Ballester's *Don Juan* (1963). The model is identified by the title itself, and the transforming process consists of the speaker's efforts to challenge the model. The anecdote involves the speaker's chance acquaintance in Paris with Leporello, a man claiming to be the servant of the famous fictional seducer. The novel, then, presents a clash between the supposed "reality" of the speaker and the living "fiction" he encounters in the form of this servant and his master. In short, the speaker inadvertently finds himself enclosed within a literary model, and his efforts to break out of that model serve as novelistic self-commentary.

The persuasiveness of the model is apparent when, after the very first encounter with Leporello, the speaker rather matter-of-factly concedes the servant's extraterrestrial ontology: "Al principio creía que iría disfrazado; ahora tengo dudas acerca de su realidad. Si hubiera de definirlo de algún modo, diría que es un fantasma"[7] ["At first I thought he was just wearing a disguise; now I have to question his reality. If I had to define him in some way, I would say he is a ghost"]. The sensation of the supernatural soon takes on a pronounced literary connotation with the narrator's first visit to Don Juan's apartment: "Leporello abrió las maderas de una ventana, y tuve la sensación repentina de hallarme en el escenario de un teatro, o en algo que, sin ser teatro, fuese escenario, y que, sin embargo, no era fingido o falso, sino de la más depurada autenticidad" (p. 29) ["Leporello opened the shutters of a window, and I suddenly felt as if I were in the middle of a theatrical scene, or in something that, although not a theatre, was a staged scene but that, nevertheless, was not contrived or false, but rather of the purest authenticity"].

A fictional setting that somehow seems real signals the convergence of the supposed real world of the narrator with the fictional world of Don Juan. Soon he begins to feel that indeed he has crossed the threshold between the two worlds, and that in so doing he has fallen under the control of the author of the fictional world: "Llegué a sentirme como juguete en sus manos, o como personaje literario en las del mal novelista, que piensa y siente lo que el novelista quiere" (p. 40) ["I came to feel like a toy in his hands, or like a literary character in the hands of a bad novelist, a character who thinks and feels what the novelist dictates"]. Since various authors (dramatists and poets as well as novelists) can claim credit for versions of the Don Juan literary legend, the model itself rather than a single author must be responsible for the dictatorial control under which the speaker has fallen. The "bad author" to whom he refers, then, seems to be a creation rather than the creator of the model. Indeed, only the speaker's fictional self-consciousness serves to counteract the stifling constraints of this all-too-familiar literary model.

Since fictional self-consciousness does seem to combat the artistic infecundity imposed by the model, the speaker decides to further the cause of creativity by usurping the role of the model's fictive author. The speaker aspires secretly to become the fictive author of his own story. Leporello, however, knows about the secret heretical project and asks permission to read the manuscript. At that point the narrator/character/author confesses that the story is silly and that he does not even know why he bothered to write it. Leporello then answers him: "Yo sí lo sé. La escribió porque no tuvo más remedio porque una fuerza superior le obligó a hacerlo. Pero no se le ocurre presumir de haberla inventado. La historia no tiene nada suyo, usted lo sabe. Ni siquiera las palabras le pertenecen" (p. 255) ["Well I do know. You wrote it because you didn't have any alternative since a force superior to you forced you to do it. But don't think you have invented it. The story is not yours at all, and you know it. The words aren't even yours"]. Leporello seems to be suggesting that the superior force is the literary model itself, that no author can free him- or herself from the constraints of tradition and reader expectations. In this sense, then, Torrente's *Don Juan* raises the questions of authorial control and artistic originality. Authors, it seems to suggest, are less creators than imitators. Torrente's *Don Juan* therefore presents the conflict between the constraints imposed by past models and formulas on any novelistic expression, and the constant need to challenge all constraints so as to express the always constant yet always changing phenomenon of human existence. The modal violation occurring when a fictional character in a contemporary novel enters the world of a classical model and then attempts to write his own story is the textual strategy by which Torrente challenges the constraints of tradition, by which he strives for a new mode of expression. So intertextuality is simultaneously an obstacle and a creative force, but for it to be creative the existing prototypes must be transformed into new modes of expression. Such seems to be the message of Torrente's *Don Juan*.

As interesting and important as Torrente's challenge to literary models is to the Spanish novel of the 1960s, it fell to another Galician novelist, Alvaro Cunqueiro, and his *Un hombre que se parecía a Orestes* (1969) [*A Man Who Resembled Orestes*], to develop more fully the potential of transforming classical archetypes into new modes of expression. In so doing Cunqueiro points even more directly to the emergence in the mid-1970s of the Spanish self-referential novel.

The title itself, *Un hombre que se parecía a Orestes*, points simultaneously to the hero of the classical model—Aeschylus's *Oresteia*—and to the departure from the model. That is to say, this hero only resembles the original. The title announces that Cunqueiro's novel is a rereading of the myth, a rereading that in turn has been read as demythification, revitalization, escapism, social criticism, a humorous blend of realism and fabulation, and finally a blend of self-conscious narrative and metatheatre.[8] The variety of interpretations the novel has inspired attests to its artistic complexity, an artistic complexity grounded in the clash between the formulas imposed by the classical model and the contemporary novel's search for new modes of expression.

The clash between rigid formulas and artistic innovation is most obvious in the novel's exterior structure. On several occasions the narrative mode is interrupted by the dramatic mode in the form of segments of two plays embedded within the novel. In addition, the novel ends with six character sketches followed by an onomastic index of the remaining characters (except for Aegisthus, who is strangely missing from both lists), and each sketch and index entry offers a new caricature of the respective personages.[9] The combination of theatrical modes of dialogue and a conclusion presented as sketches and indices clashes with what is conceived as traditional novelistic form. These nonconventional devices call attention to themselves as artifices, and such a flaunting of artifices is the most blatant expression of the conflict between the tyranny of literary models and the need to challenge such a tyranny. The challenge involves turning the conventions and artifices against themselves. First by exaggerating the rigidity of generic formulas and then by violating the very modes of literature, the novel offers a new set of formulas and models to express in contemporary terms an ancient conflict of human existence.

The conflict between original model and modern imitation is central to the anecdote of *Un hombre que se parecía a Orestes*. When the novel begins a stranger has arrived in the city, introducing himself as Don León. Since the people of the city have been waiting for a long time for the arrival of Orestes and a spy network has been set up to identify him and prevent his murderous revenge, all strangers are suspect. Yet as Don León's words, actions, and physical appearance suggest more and more that he is indeed the avenging hero, the people become increasingly skeptical of the whole myth. In fact, as the captain of the spy network explains, the situation has taken on an aura of play acting: "Y ellos, los reyes, no podrán morir si no viene Orestes. El pueblo estará ese día como en el teatro"[10] ["And they, the king and queen, will not be able to die if Orestes does not come. That day everyone will feel as if he is at the theatre"]. The people, in short, feel that their own identity is determined by the fictional model, yet this identity is in conflict with their present context, a context totally lacking the epic dimensions associated with the model: "¡Coño, eso parece de la tragedia!—había comentado Eusebio. Pero él cobraba por descubrir a Orestes, y debía registrar al forastero que le señalaban en el aviso" (p. 25) ["Motherfucker, that business sounds as if it's right out of the tragedy—Eusebio had commented. But they paid him to investigate Orestes, and he had to check out the stranger described in the bulletin"]. Not only does the vulgarity underscore the degree to which pragmatic considerations have supplanted the cosmic forces behind the original myth, but the same vulgar pragmatism reflects how the myth has been reduced to mere formulas. Rather than a fiction, it is an anti-fiction suppressing both compassion and imagination.

The anti-fiction resulting when fiction is reduced to a rigid set of norms becomes evident when one of the city augurs responds to Don León's question about the theatre offerings currently available:

Yo también soy muy amigo del teatro, don León, pero a los augures nos está prohibido en esta ciudad, ya que el pueblo respetuoso teme que estando nosotros en los tendidos viendo la pieza, apasionados por el protagonista, o de una mujer hermosa que salga, hagamos suertes a escondidas dentro de una bolsa con habas blancas y dientes de liebre, y modifiquemos el curso de la tragedia, y llegue a anciano respetable un incestuoso, o Medea reconquiste a Jasón, y todo quede en besos a los niños. [p. 41]

[I am also a theatre buff, Don León, but we augurs are prohibited from seeing it in this city, since the respectable people are afraid that if we are in the balcony watching the play, and become caught up by the protagonist, or by some beautiful woman who happens onto the stage, we may secretly throw dice made of white beans and rabbit teeth in a bag, and thereby change the course of the tragedy, and an incestuous person will achieve respectable old age, or Medea may reconquer Jason, and in the end everyone will be just one big happy family.]

The characters, therefore, are slaves to all past literary models. They cannot escape the model they are in, and are prohibited from using their creative imagination to alter other models. And whereas such exaggeration of their enslavement produces a comic effect, it also tends to reduce the literary work to its anecdotal level; it presents literature as nothing more than a finite number of plot situations, each so rigidly defined that plot is seen as another of the arbitrary conventions constraining literature's ability to express the ever-changing yet ever-constant essence of human existence.

Literature as convention becomes even more evident with the first example of a play within the novel. The official city dramatist, Filón el Mozo, has defied the law by secretly writing a theatrical version of Orestes' appearance. After a textual reproduction of Scene One, Scene Two of Filón's play begins and then abruptly ends at the moment Iphigenia looks out the window and is supposed to see Orestes. At this point the dramatic form gives way to the narrative form as the speaker intrudes to explain that the dramatist cannot finish the scene until Orestes actually arrives. In addition to mocking the conventions of plot, the mixture of dramatic and narrative fictional forms comically lays bare the illusion that fiction is about real people, places, and events. Not only do we have fiction within fiction, but the referent on which the completion of Filón's play depends is itself a fiction; the fictitious scene representing the arrival of Orestes cannot be written until Orestes (a fictional character) makes his appearance. Thus Filón's absurd fidelity to mimetic art directs attention to the absurdity of ever thinking that art and reality are one. Only conventions allow us to accept fiction as real. In short, this segment of a play within the novel comically exaggerates the conventions of fiction, and in so doing turns them against themselves. Rather than absolute laws, they reveal themselves to be arbitrary constraints or formulas badly in need of revitalization.

Since true revitalization demands certain commitments, the characters opt instead for embellishment. Filón el Mozo, for example, contents himself with imagining embellishments for Orestes' arrival scene, since he is unwilling to write his own ending. Even Aegisthus follows Filón's example as he dreams of ways to adorn the scene of his own murder:

Egisto, verdaderamente, lo pensaba todo como si la escena final se desarrollase en el teatro, ante cientos o miles de espectadores. Un día se dio cuenta de que Clitemnestra tenía que estar presente en todo el último acto, esperando su hora. Podría Egisto, en la pared del fondo, en el dormitorio, mandar abrir un ventanal sobre la sala de embajadores, un ventanal que permitiese ver la cama matrimonial, y en ella a Clitemnestra en camisón, la cabellera dorada derramada en la almohada, los redondos hombros desnudos. Cuando se incorporase, despertada por el ruido de las armas, en el sobresalto debía mostrar los pechos, e intentando abandonar el lecho para correr hacia el ventanal, una de las hermosas piernas hasta medio muslo, o algo más, que la tragedia permite todo lo que el terror exige. [pp. 79-80]

[Aegisthus really conceived of the whole thing as if the final scene were unfolding in the theatre, before hundreds or thousands of spectators. One day he realized that Clytemnestra had to be present during all the final act, waiting for her time. Aegisthus could have a bay window over the ambassadors' waiting room opened, on the wall in the background of the bedroom, a bay window that would allow the marital bed to be seen, and on it Clytemnestra in a chemise, her blonde hair spread out over the pillow, her round shoulders bare. When she gets up, awakened by the noise of the weapons, in her excitement she should bare her breasts, and in the process of attempting to get out of bed and run to the bay window, also one of her legs up to mid-thigh, or perhaps a little higher, for in theatre you can get away with whatever the dramatic situation requires.]

The embellishment he imagines, of course, merely transforms an epic tragedy into a titillating soap opera. Although he is a self-conscious fictional character and frustrated with his formulaic existence, his action here represents at best a half-hearted rebellion against the formulas; by ridiculously embellishing them, he underscores their authority over him.

True rebellion, as he learns from his friend Eumón, requires a much more radical approach. Eumón suggests the radical solution when he learns from Aegisthus that no one who knew Agamemnon saw the face of the victim after the murder. Eumón then speculates that the victim was actually Orestes who, impatiently waiting for his father to be murdered, arrived before the crime was committed, and thus Aegisthus erroneously killed the son rather than the father. According to Eumón, it is simply a matter of changing the story's sequence of events:

Fíjate en que todo está escrito. Todo lo que está escrito en un libro, lo está al mismo tiempo, vive al mismo tiempo. Estás leyendo que Eumón sale de Tracia una mañana de lluvia, y lo ves cabalgar por aquel camino que va entre tojales, y pasas de repente veinte hojas, y ya está Eumón en una nave, y otras veinte y Eumón pasea por Constantinopla con un quitasol, y otras cincuenta, y Eumón, anciano, en su lecho de muerte, se despide de sus perros favoritos, al tiempo que vuelve a la página primera, recordando la dulce lluvia de su primer viaje. Pues bien, Orestes se sale de página. Orestes está impaciente. No quiere estar en la página ciento cincuenta esperando a que llegue la hora de la venganza. Se va a adelantar. [p. 98]

[You have to realize that everything is written down. Everything that is written down in a book takes place at the same time, exists at the same time. You are reading that Eumón leaves Thrace one rainy morning, and you see him riding along that road bordered by furze trees, and you suddenly skip twenty pages, and Eumón is now on a boat, and another twenty and Eumón strolls through Constantinople with a parasol, and another fifty pages and he is now an old man on his death bed, and is saying goodbye to his favorite dogs, at the very same time that his mind skips back to the first page, remembering the sweet rain that was falling as he left on his first excursion. Well, Orestes is leaving his place on the page. Orestes is impatient. He doesn't want to be on page one hundred and fifty waiting for the time of his vengeance. He is going to hurry things along.]

Eumón's solution does not merely question the conventions of plot, it challenges the very laws of fiction. In effect he exposes fiction as a totally arbitrary game that pretends that space and sequential order represent temporal progression. Aegisthus, or any other artist, has the power to change the rules of the game. Yet the rebellion implicit in changing the rules does involve certain consequences, for as Aegisthus reasons, his own role in the tragedy will be diminished if the victim was Orestes rather than Agamemnon. Eumón quickly tries to dispel his friend's apprehensions: "¡Tu valor no se discute, amigo!—afirmó Eumón abrazándolo—. ¡Ya verás como si profundizas en el asunto, terminas saliendo del escenario para platea, ves el argumento con nuevos ojos y acabas separando de ti el Egisto regicida!" (p. 102) ["Your valor is beyond challenge, my friend!—Eumón affirmed hugging him. You will soon see, if you delve into the matter more, that you will finally come down off the stage and take a place in the orchestra seats, where you will see the plot from a whole new perspective and will end up separating from yourself the regicidal Aegisthus."] After first exposing the artifices of fiction, he now is attempting to incite to riot a fellow fictional character by encouraging him to defy the authority of the fictive author Aeschylus. Eumón's advice represents a violation of narrative modes. Yet the violation occurs within the embedded text. By advocating to Aegisthus that he step out of Aeschylus's fictional world, in effect he is encouraging him to place himself under the authority of the fictive author of the framing text. He is being encouraged to substitute the *persona* of Cunqueiro for that of Aeschylus. If he does so he will become a new Aegisthus ("acabas separando de ti el Egisto regicida") contributing, of course, to Cunqueiro's new reading of the ancient myth.

Eumón's rebellious advice to violate the embedded text's narrative boundaries is, in the final analysis, a vital part of Cunqueiro's textual strategy for revitalizing fictional modes. Rather than a novel that pretends to mirror reality or that slavishly follows established norms, this novel mirrors itself by challenging fictional norms. Yet ultimately Aegisthus rejects the advice and chooses to continue his sterile, formulaic existence. Authentic rebellion is left in the hands of the protagonist of the second of Filón el Mozo's plays, Doña Inés.

Doña Inés is the protagonist of Azorín's famous novel of the same title published in 1925. In that novel Doña Inés, approaching middle age, falls victim to her own romantic idealism, which comes in conflict with a prosaic, pragmatic world. The literary name Doña Inés is thus identified with tragic, unrequited love. The Doña Inés of Cunqueiro's novel lives in an adjoining kingdom, and when Eumón learns that she is the referent for Filón's theatrical heroine, Eumón cannot resist a little spicy gossip: "— Me dice Egisto en confianza—explicó Eumón a Filón el Mozo—, que todo el desequilibrio de doña Inés viene de estar ella también a la espera de Orestes, sólo que para recibirlo con cama deshecha" (p. 167) ["Aegisthus tells me confidentially—Eumón explained to

Filón el Mozo—, that all of Doña Inés's emotional problems can be explained because she is also waiting for Orestes, only in her case to greet him in bed with the covers thrown back"]. Such a lascivious remark humorously mocks the very romantic ideals associated with the name Doña Inés. It is the first step in departing from the model, in offering a new reading, in this case of a modern, rather than an ancient, classic. In fact, reading itself becomes the primary focus with the interpolation of this second play within the novel.

The focus begins to switch from the story to reading and readers when Eumón asks permission to read Filón el Mozo's play about Doña Inés. With the subsequent appearance of the dramatic mode, then, it is not a question of the illusion of real-life drama, but rather of the convention of written dramatic form. The dramatic mode appearing on the page represents the text Eumón holds in his hand.

The initial scenes Eumón reads concern the arrival of a mailman at Doña Inés's castle and the story the mailman fabricates to explain why he has no love letters for her. The explanation he offers is that a handsome prince called him aside in Florence and, continually glancing at his watch, asked him to tell Doña Inés that he would write her declaring his love as soon as he had time to do so. Doña Inés then takes the mailman's watch and, holding it to her ear, cries that its ticking is the very love message she has been awaiting. With this ending to the scene, there is an abrupt switch from the dramatic to the narrative mode: "Eumón de Tracia sacó su reloj y lo escuchó y se dijo que sería muy hermoso el tener un amor lejano y saber de él así. Y se dolió de sí mismo, que nunca lo habían amado tanto, ni se le habían ocurrido tales imaginaciones amorosas" (p. 178) ["Eumón of Thrace took out his watch and listened to it, and he said to himself that it would be beautiful to have a distant love and to hear about her that way. And he felt sorry for himself because he had never been loved that much, nor had he even dreamed such amorous thoughts"]. With the change of mode, suddenly the focus falls on Eumón as a reader of fiction rather than merely a character in it. By expanding the vision from the embedded text to the framing text, the text-act reader is signaled that the fictional mode involves not only a story but an implied reader of the story. The shift of focus suddenly reveals the role of Eumón as a text reader; it makes explicit what is conventionally an implicit dimension of the fictional mode.

This example of modal shift, moreover, lays bare not only the convention of the implied text reader but also that of a suspension of disbelief. By changing the focus from what is represented to the person reacting to the representation, the convention of a suspension of disbelief is turned against itself. Eumón, in his reaction to the play, is even more ridiculous than Doña Inés. Thus, rather than an enticement to accept fiction as reality, Cunqueiro's textual strategy is an invitation to contemplate how the illusions of reality depend on the comically arbitrary rules by which the game we call fiction is played.

The culmination of the process of turning the conventions of fiction against themselves, of rebelling against the constraints of both genre and mode, involves the recognition by Doña Inés of her purely linguistic-artistic ontology. When a musician visits Doña Inés in her tower and, after boasting how he creates reality with his music, challenges her reality by questioning if she is really the mistress of the castle, she indignantly responds:

¿Podría serlo otro? Yo soy el palacio, este palacio, este jardín, este bosque, este reino. A veces imagino que me marcho, que abandono el palacio en la noche, que huyo sin despedirme, y conforme lo voy imaginando siento que la casa se estremece, que amenazan quebrarse las vigas, se desgoznan las puertas, se agrietan las paredes, y parece que todo vaya a derrumbarse en un repente, y caer, reducido a polvo y escombro, en el suelo. Todo esto depende de mí, músico, de esta frase que soy yo, en una larga sinfonía repetida monótonamente, ahora adagio, después allegro, alguna vez andante. [p. 180]

[Could it be anyone else? I am the palace, this palace, this garden, this forest, this kingdom. At times I imagine that I am leaving, that I am abandoning the palace during the night, that I am fleeing without saying goodby, and as I imagine it I feel that the house shudders, that the beams threaten to split, that the doors come loose from their hinges, that the walls crack, and it seems as if everything is suddenly going to crumble and fall, reduced to dust and rubble on the ground. All this depends on me, musician, on this series of sounds that I am, in a long symphony, first adagio, then allegro, once in a while andante.]

Initially she merely seems to be affirming her ownership of the property when she says she *is* the palace, garden, forest, and kingdom. The meaning becomes more complex, however, when she speaks of the destruction accompanying her imagined departures from the tower. The key to decoding the meaning seems to be provided by her self-definition as a "frase." Within the anecdotal context the word "frase" seems to indicate a musical phrase, one of its dictionary definitions. Yet within the structural context of a fiction within a fiction, the word "frase" also points at its more common meaning as a grammatical unit. In either case the use of the word reflects Doña Inés's awareness of being part of an artistic work. In fact, not only she but everything surrounding her is but a verbal construct, a constituent part of an artistic whole. If one of the constituent parts decides to rebel, therefore, the artistic whole may well crumble. Her self-awareness of the role she plays distinguishes her from all the other characters appearing in the novel. She is aware not only of her fictionality but also of her capacity to rebel, and finally is willing to face the consequences of such a rebellion, consequences that in effect challenge the very concept of artistic unity. Self-awareness of this magnitude violates the modes of fiction, for Doña Inés not only is destroying any illusion that she is a real person but is also rebelling against the literary model associated with her name, against the creator of that model, and finally against the very concept of absolute unity.

At first glance the section of *Un hombre que se parecía a Orestes* dedicated to Doña Inés seems to be an artistic infelicity; it appears to destroy the novel's structural and thematic unity. Yet I would argue that, on the contrary, it can be seen as an essential link in the novel's redefinition of artistic unity.[11] Doña Inés's appearance in a novel about Orestes in itself represents a defiance of literary models; she is a characater from a modern novel invading the world of a Greek classic. Because of her role as intruder, along with her self-awareness of her linguistic-artistic ontology, Doña Inés represents the realization of a rebellion the other characters are unwilling to attempt. In fact, Doña Inés functions as a sign pointing toward artistic freedom. By recognizing herself as a convention or an artifice, she turns that convention or artifice against itself in a dramatic expression of novelistic self-commentary. The story of Doña Inés can be seen, therefore, as a fitting culmination to the central conflict of the novel, a conflict between the constraints of established conventions and models, and the need to find new means of artistic expression, new strategies for revitalizing ancient and modern myths, new readings of our literary tradition.

Un hombre que se parecía a Orestes represents a significant step toward the Spanish self-referential novel emerging in the mid 1970s. Cunqueiro, while still relying on parody and the foregrounding of literary codes (strategies that seem to carry the imprint of Jarnés on them), places major emphasis on a violation of the modes of fiction. The novelistic self-commentary, therefore, concerns the underlying laws of fiction more than mere stylistic constraints. Yet even his violations are only partial. When Eumón preaches rebellion to Aegisthus and Doña Inés does rebel by recognizing her artistic ontology, both are violating the boundary separating them as characters from the world of their respective fictive authors. But the violations are of the world of the fictive authors of the embedded texts. In the final analysis they are rebelling against the *personae* of Aeschylus and Azorín only to place themselves under the authority of Cunqueiro's *persona*. The boundaries of the framing text remain intact. In short, Cunqueiro artfully controls the metafictional mode so as to serve the cause of a novelistic expression that, while not pretending to duplicate, still resembles its classical models.

With the emergence of the new self-referential novel in the mid 1970s, the Spanish novel becomes much more radical in its violations and much more concerned with fiction's modes of existence. Indeed, rather than merely exposing the artifices of fiction, the new genre foregrounds its own process of creation, its own coming-into-being. The conventions of narrative levels are all but annihilated as what is narrated and the narrating instance tend to fuse. While I am not suggesting that Alvaro Cunqueiro's *Un hombre que se parecía a Orestes* had a direct influence on the Spanish self-referential novelists, certainly it played a role in shaping reader expectations for the new metafictional movement. At the very least Cunqueiro's novel forms a link in an intertextual chain that helps us as critics to recognize more clearly, and perhaps appreciate more deeply, some of the techniques involved and effects created by the new wave of Spanish metafictional novels.

Chapter Five

Process as Product: *Juan sin Tierra*

When, metafiction is defined as a mode, as proposed in the Introduction to this study, it forms a polar opposite to reportorial fiction. That is to say, the reportorial mode points almost directly at extratextual reality while the metafictional mode tends to point back at the work itself. Both modes, nevertheless, can appear in the same novel, as indeed is the case in numerous examples from Galdós. (While not exactly the reportorial mode, Galdosian realism is close to it.) Furthermore, since modes are atemporal, we find dramatic examples of the metafictional mode from *Don Quijote* to the present. Yet prior to the last decade in Spain, the mode appeared sporadically, generally as a mutation of other generic movements. And when it did appear it served to foreground the artifices and conventions of fiction; it switched the focus from the created image to the strategies involved in creating it. In short, the novels examined up to this point in which the metafictional mode plays a significant role convey a fascination with fiction as a weaver of dreams.

In the decade of the 1970s not only did the metafictional mode begin to dominate in specific novels, but such novels became the dominant force in the field of Spanish fiction. The mode finally gave birth to a general novelistic movement which I have labeled the Spanish self-referential novel.[1] Certainly one could argue that the switch to such a term at this juncture merely adds confusion to an already confusing issue. Yet I would counterargue, echoing what I tried to demonstrate at the beginning of this study, that much of the confusion surrounding the term metafiction stems from the historical misuse of the terms mode and genre. Since I have been using metafiction up to this point to refer to an atemporal mode of expression, the danger of confusion would be even greater if I were now to use the same term to label a temporally-bound body of texts. The term Spanish self-referential Novel, moreover, is designed not only to address the mode-genre issue but to reflect the fact that the current expression of the mode does not lead to the same effects seen so far in this study. Rather than foregrounding the artifices and conventions of fiction, the self-referential novel foregrounds the process of its own creation; more than a novel about fiction, it is a novel about its own coming-into-being. In short, the self-referential novel conveys a fascination with the creative process itself.

With the emregence of a whole movement in which metafiction is the predominant mode, the question of categories and divisions within the movement arises. Since categories and divisions inevitably reflect the critical approach applied, what I am about to propose is a reflection of my focus on the concept of modes, and of my basic definition of metafiction as a violation of fictional modes. Another critical approach and another basic definition of metafiction would perhaps lead to a different body of texts and to different categories and divisions within it. Again, then, I am not attempting to pigeonhole but rather to propose a vision, one way of looking at a selected group of texts. In no way do I wish to suggest that it is the only way of looking at such a group.

With the preceding caveat underscored, the Spanish self-referential novel falls into three basic categories or divisions: those focusing on the world of the fictive author (the act of writing), those focusing on the world of the fictive reader (the act of reading), and those focusing on the world of the characters and actions (the act of oral discoursing). Naturally the focus in any given group of novels does not fall exclusively on any one of the three worlds—such an exclusiveness of focus would probably be impossible. Yet the concentration on one world at the expense of the other two is one distinguishing characteristic of the Spanish self-referential novels of the 1970s and 1980s. The subsequent chapters will demonstrate how various novels tend to group themselves according to one of the three foci mentioned as they foreground their own process of creation.

The first Spanish novel not only associating itself with a focus on the act of writing, but marking the beginning of the general self-referential movement of the 1970s, is Luis Goytisolo's *Recuento* (1973) [*Recount*].[2] In fact, it is the first novel of a tetralogy entitled *Antagonía* [*Antagonism*], all four works of which are keystones of the self-referential movement.

In its initial chapters, *Recuento* seems to teeter on a line between neorealism and the New Novel. In either case the focus is on the story, and the act of narrating is limited to the traces it leaves on what is narrated. In the final chapters, however, the focus shifts from the product to the process of narrating:

No obstante, ya en el curso del primer capítulo, las descripciones deben ir perdiendo su carácter objetivo, casi enunciativo. Se irán haciendo subjetivas, irreales, en cierto modo. Como los paisajes que uno imagina al contemplar las nubes desde un avión. Repeticiones contradictorias. En los capítulos siguientes, lo mismo que los diálogos, desaparecerán paulatinamente. [p. 638]

[Nevertheless, already in the course of the first chapter the descriptions should slowly begin to lose their objective, almost enunciative, character. They will slowly become subjective, unreal, in a certain sense. Like the landscapes that one imagines when looking at clouds from an airplane. Contradictory repetitions. In the subsequent chapters, just like the dialogues, they will gradually disappear.]

As the novel draws to an end the fictive author becomes so self-conscious that he not only analyzes what he has already written, but speculates as to how he should write the subsequent pages, a speculation that points directly at the next novel in the tetralogy. The end of *Recuento*, therefore, is no longer about Raúl or the story of his physical-psychological development, but about the process involved in writing his story. Thus *Recuento* not only marks the beginning of the Spanish self-referential novel, but is also the first of a series of novels focusing on the world of the fictive author and his act of writing his own novel.

Whereas the act of writing is foregrounded only near the end of *Recuento*, it serves as the principal focus for Luis Goytisolo's next novel, *Los verdes de mayo hasta el mar* (1976) [*The Verdure of May All the Way to the Sea*].[3] In this second work of the tetralogy, the story concerns Raúl as he is writing a novel while vacationing in Rosas on the Costa Brava. The line separating the novel Raúl is writing from the story of his writing it, however, continually shifts. Raúl finds the referents for his novel in his own context, and then transforms them into fictional entities. But as the process unfolds and the focus shifts constantly from Raúl's context to the novel he is creating, the two worlds become confused; characters from Raúl's world appear, untransformed, in the novel he is writing, and the fictitious characters from the novel appear in his world. Finally the focus shifts to the act of narrating as a means of clarifying this confusion between the author's context and the novel he is writing:

recopilación de las notas tomadas por el protagonista durante su estancia en Rosas respecto a una obra en curso, entremezcladas a otras anotaciones, recuerdos, reflexiones, comentarios referentes a su vida cotidiana, etcétera; un relato que, al tiempo que refiere la anécdota cotidiana del protagonista y su mujer o amante en Rosas, incluye, junto a las anotaciones relativas a una obra que está escribiendo, así como reflexiones, recuerdos, etcétera, las anotaciones relativas a la anécdota de esa estancia en Rosas, recreación de la realidad con todas las deformaciones y transposiciones que le son propias y que, a la vez que proyección del protagonista sobre la realidad, sobre una realidad a la que éste atribuye todas sus obsesiones personales, suponen asimismo una incidencia de la obra en el autor, tanto por lo que sobre sí mismo le revelan cuanto por lo que le velan. Yuxtaponer, o mejor, superponer a la variante óptima diversos materiales pertenecientes al resto de las variantes. [pp. 256-57]

[summary of the notes taken by the protagonist during his stay at Rosas in respect to a work in progress, mixed in with other notations, memories, ruminations, comments concerning his daily life, etc.; a story that, at the same time that it refers to the everyday anecdote of the protagonist and his wife or lover in Rosas, includes, along with the notations relative to a work that is being written, as well as ruminations, memories, etc., the notations relative to the anecdote of the stay in Rosas, a recreation of reality with all its deformations and transpositions that are a part of it and that, at the same time that it is a projection of the protagonist into reality, into a reality to which he attributes all his personal obsessions, these deformations and transpositions presuppose also a point of incidence of the work and the author, not only concerning what they reveal of him, but also what they hide. Juxtapose, or better, superimpose on the best variation of the work diverse materials pertaining to the rest of the variations.]

Obviously the clarification is as confusing as the process it pretends to explain, if not more so. It does, however, convey the problem of the referent vis-à-vis the creative process. The levels of fiction which initially were relatively clear—Raúl in Rosas writing a novel about a protagonist in Rosas—become impossibly intertwined as the fictive author tries to convey how Raúl, the character/novelist, attempts to transform referents from his world into the novel he is writing. In addition, the character/novelist's act of writing within the fiction becomes intertwined with the fictive author's act of writing the fiction. Reality, therefore, is a point of departure that soon is impossible to define: "la intersección o incidencia de los distintos planos—real uno, ficticio el otro, ficticiamente real un tercero, y así siguiendo" (pp. 266-67) ["the intersection or point of incidence of distinct levels—one real, the other fictitious, a third fictitiously real, and so on"]. In *Los verdes de mayo hasta el mar* it becomes impossible to distinguish between one level of fiction and another, or even between reality and fiction. Indeed, reality in this novel obviously cannot be equated with geographical or proper names, characters, dates, and events, but with the process itself of writing fiction. Stated in another way, the act of narrating is real; the product or what is narrated is always a fiction.

Los verdes de mayo hasta el mar, then, reflects the shift from the product to the process of creating the product initiated near the end of *Recuento*. Thus these two novels, along with José María Merino's *Novela de Andrés Choz* (1977) [*Andrés Choz's Novel*], in which there is also a character/novelist writing a novel, form the nucleus of a group of Spanish self-referential novels focusing on the world of the fictive author, on the process of writing. Yet the work that most dramatically foregrounds the narrating instance is written by the brother of Luis, Juan Goytisolo. Indeed, *Juan sin Tierra* (1975)[4] [*Juan the Landless* in the English version] could well be considered the manifesto for the whole Spanish self-referential novel movement.

Juan sin Tierra violates the laws of fiction by challenging the very distinction between the world *from* which one narrates and the world *of* which one narrates. In fact, the process and the product of narrating alternately determine and are determined by one another. The text author constantly interrupts his narration to contemplate what he has created, and what he has created dictates his next step in the creative process.[5] The text author, therefore, is both the creator and the creation of his own artistic efforts. *Juan sin Tierra*, as a result, foregrounds the act of writing becoming the novel at hand, and the text author becoming a new kind of novelist—although within the work this dual coming-into-being is a simultaneous process.

Since *Juan sin Tierra* is an example of art-in-process, the novel's referent is itself. Indeed, the text author's expressed purpose is to free the work and its language from their traditional denotative function:

autonomía del objeto literario : estructura verbal con sus propias relaciones internas, lenguaje percibido en sí mismo y no como intercesor transparente de un mundo ajeno, exterior : mediante el acto de liberar las palabras de su obediencia a un orden pragmático que las convierte en meros vehículos de la razón omnímoda : de un pensamiento lógico que desdeñosamente las utiliza sin tener en cuenta su peso específico y su valor : completando las funciones de representación, expresión y llamada inherentes a una comunicación oral cuyos elementos (emisor, receptor, contexto, contacto) operan también (aunque de modo diverso) en el instante de la lectura con una cuarta función (erógena?) que centrará exclusivamente su atención en el signo lingüístico : descargando, gracias a ella, al lenguaje de su simoníaca finalidad ancillar[6]

[autonomy of the literary object : a verbal structure with its own internal relationships, a language perceived in itself and not as a transparent conduit of a separated, exterior world : by means of the act of liberating the words from their obedience to a pragmatic order that converts them into mere vehicles of absolute reason : of a logical thought that disdainfully uses them without considering their specific weight and value : completing the functions of representation, expression and appellation inherent to an oral communication whose elements (addresser, addressee, context, contact) also operate (although in a diverse mode) in the instant of reading with a fourth function (erogenous?) which will center its attention exclusively on the linguistic sign : freeing, thanks to it, language from its false ancillary finality.]

This example of self-conscious narration—perhaps more accurately self-conscious theorizing about the act of narrating—occurs in the final chapter of the novel, a chapter in which the focus is centered exclusively on the narrating instance. That is, in the final chapter the world *of* which one narrates is totally supplanted by the world *from* which one narrates; rather than merely a violation of the boundaries separating the two worlds, the worlds in effect change places. Such a transposition (in which the act of writing obliterates what is written, or the story) represents the culmination of a process in which the two—the act of writing and its product—vie for dominant position. The textual strategy underlying such a conflict involves transforming cultural codes into narrative codes,[7] of freeing language from externally-imposed meaning so that it may develop its own internal relationships and the ultimate "autonomy of the literary object."

In order to transform cultural codes into narrative codes, the text author creates a series of binary oppositions. The first of such binary oppositions involves non-body versus body as the text author attempts to transcend the limitations of his physical existence. In his quest to reach a state of nirvana, he suddenly realizes that humans can never negate their bodies: "cuerpo tan sólo : despliegue de materia : hijo de la tierra y a la tierra unido" (p. 11) [mere flesh : an extension of matter : child of the earth and inseparable from the earth"]. This initial opposition expands into a whole sign system whose axis is formed by the anecdotal conflict sometime during the nineteenth century between the text author's white Spanish ancestors and their black Cuban slaves.

The white colonizers-black slaves dichotomy is culturally precoded: ascetic Judeo-Christian values for the whites versus pagan sensual gratification for the blacks. But as this cultural coding expands, the text author suddenly interrupts what he is narrating to focus on his act of narrating, and to advise himself as to the next step: "dividirás la imaginaria escena en dos partes : dicho mejor : en dos bloques opuestos de palabras : a un lado substantivos, adjetivos, verbos que denotan blancor, claridad, virtud : al otro, un léxico de tinieblas, negrura, pecado" (p. 30) ["you will divide the imaginary scene into two parts : more accurately : into two opposing blocks of words : on one side nouns, adjectives, verbs signifying whiteness, clarity, virtue : on the other, a lexicon of shadows, blackness, sin"]. With this violation of the story by the act of narrating, the original cultural codes become narrative; what were originally objects from sociohistorical reality have been transformed into linguistic signs guiding the text author in his search for a new, freer mode of novelistic expression. He has taken the first step toward freeing language from externally-imposed meaning.

The liberation of language also occurs on the anecdotal level. When the priest Vosk looks out the plantation house window to spy on the slaves' activities, and is too horrified to describe to the good Catholic family what he sees, he is told to explain it in Latin:

> membrum erectum in os feminae immissint!
> socios concumbentes tangere et masturbationem mutuam adsequi!
> penis vehementis se erixet tum maxime cum crura
> puerorum tetigent!
> anus feminarum amant lambere!
> sanguinis menstruationis devorant!
> coitus a posterioris factitant!
> ejaculatio praematura!
> receptaculum seminis! [p. 32]

Since spoken Latin is largely restricted to use within the Church, its effect here demonstrates the influence of cultural codes on semantics. Although the description involves sexual activities that would scandalize Vosk's text addressees (the text author's ancestors), the sound produced by the liturgical rhythm of the Latin erases the words' meaning for them. The message implicit in this combination of what the words mean and how the family decodes them triggers another switch to the narrating instance: "interrupción, oquedad, silencio : como cuando dejas de escribir" (p. 32) ["interruption, hollowness, silence : as when you stop writing"]. Apparently the text author, who in effect is his own text-act reader, finds in this scene a message concerning the arbitrary nature of language, and how easily its meaning can be subverted. His response is to create more subversive binary oppositions.

The metonymic expansion of subversive oppositions evolves soon into the flush toilet versus the open-air latrine. The flush toilet is coded by virtue of its location in the plantation home, where its use is strictly limited to the white masters. In addition, this new sanitary device points back to the original non-body-versus-body opposition, and to the subversive conflict between semantics and context, as the text author's great-grandmother satisfies her needs: "tirará de la cadena oculta en el bordaje del palio y, cerrando los ojos con místico arrobo, murmurará para sí / he cagado como una reina" (pp. 19-20) ["she will pull the handle hidden at the side of the tank and, closing her eyes in a mystical trance, murmur almost to herself / I've just shit like a queen"]. Contrasted to this humorous mixture of scatological vulgarity and regal pretensions on the part of the white mistress is the black slaves' response to being ridiculed by their masters:

abrumados por el peso de la vergüenza, girarán sobre sus talones y os volverán dignamente la espalda sin conseguir otra cosa que revelar a la estupefacta asamblea la humillante coloración de sus hemisferios posteriores : la no-sublimada, no-oculta, no-inodora, no aséptica explosión visceral que ninguna caja de caudales, sagrario o WC logrará escamotear. [p. 46]

[overcome by the weight of their embarrassment, they will spin on their heels and turn their backs on you with dignity, merely achieving in the process the view for the stupefied gathering of the humiliating coloration of their posterior hemispheres : the nonsublimated, nonhidden, nonodorless, nonaseptic intestinal explosion that no safe-deposit box, sanctuary, or flush toilet will manage to snatch away by sleight of hand.]

Their retort is not only totally natural for them but appropriately vulgar. They are accustomed to satisfying their digestive functions in a public open-air latrine, while the white masters use the flush toilet as a means of denying their identical functions.[8]

The Spaniards' inclination to equate Christianity with nonbody eventually leads to an attempt to suppress completely all bodily secretions, and when the speaker imagines himself as a small boy seated on a chamber pot and being encouraged by his parents to resist his body's demands, the narrated story is again interrupted: "(el) dompedro te orienta quizá por la buena vía y te inspira de paso la solución : la de un país (el suyo) secularmente estreñido" (p. 226) ["the chamber pot perhaps points out to you the right path and in the process inspires your solution : that of a country (his) secularly constipated"]. Again story level cedes to the narrating instance; the culturally-coded sanitary devices now are narratively-coded signs pointing toward a new kind of writing:

ah, y sobre todo, abandonar inmediatamente el uso del dompedro o WC automático en favor de la desdeñada evacuación ancestral! : una posición defectuosa durante el proceso constituye un obstáculo grave a la oportuna liberación del intestino : en lugar de acomodarse en un asiento horizontal a cuarenta centímetros del suelo (o algo menos de la mitad en el caso del dompedro) el sujeto (o país) estreñido debe ponerse en cuclillas, apoyando de preferencia los pies en un escalón elevado, de una altura de veinticinco centímetros : dicha postura (se lo garantizamos!) coadyuva al funcionamiento de los músculos abdominales que impulsan la circulación serpentina y constituye un argumento de peso en boca de quienes preconizan la óptima relajación del canal y el retorno a los viejos, entrañables placeres de la emisión de la zanja pública. (p. 228)

[ah, and above all abandon immediately the use of the chamber pot or flush toilet in favor of the discredited ancestral means of evacuation! : a defective position during the process constitutes a grave obstacle to the opportune liberation of the intestine : instead of positioning oneself on a horizontal seat forty centimeters from the floor (or a bit less than half the distance in the case of the chamber pot) the constipated subject (or country) should squat down, preferably supporting his feet on an elevated step, at a height of twenty-five centimeters : such a posture (we guarantee you!) facilitates the function of the abdominal muscles that set in motion the serpentine circulation and constitutes a strong argument for those who champion the optimum relaxation of the intestinal tract and the return to the old, dear pleasures of emission in a public open-air latrine.]

The story of the Spanish white colonizers versus the Cuban black slaves has been supplanted by the act of narrating. Each sign evolves from the signs preceding it, and at the same time inspires yet another sign in response. From non-body versus body, from white versus black, from semantics versus context, and now from flush toilet versus open-air latrine, the system inevitably leads to the narrating instance. The novel is about its own creative process, a creative process grounded in binary oppositions.

The expanding system of oppositions leads to even more implausible pairings as a "Reproductive Couple" and Shirley Temple appear on the one hand, opposed by a homosexual couple and King Kong on the other. Within the first dichotomy the text author projects himself as a character in the story, and attacks and homosexually violates a wretched beggar in full view of American, Italian, French, and Spanish tourists in Tangiers. This scandalous non-propagating sexual conduct is contrasted with the "sanctified" activities of the Spanish "Reproductive Couple" who, as if they are mannequins, mechanically perform their coupling in the show window of a large department store. They are trying valiantly to comply with their Christian obligation to propagate the species. The transformation of these culturally grounded characters into signs pointing at the act of writing occurs when the Spanish couple's product-oriented efforts are frustrated by impotency:[9] "la tribulación de la Parejita resulta cada vez más lastimosa y en vano repetirán gerundios e imperativos : irregular, quizás defectivo, el verbo no alzará" (p. 73) ["the Couple's distress is becoming more and more pitiful and in vain they will repeat gerunds, and imperatives : irregular, perhaps defective, the verb won't rise erect"].

The relationship between creative impotency and judeo-Christian values culminates with the appearance of the blonde Shirley Temple. Her polar opposite is a grotesque figure from popular cinema, the black ape King Kong. The actress is an example of a real person transformed by cinema into a symbol of Western cultural values; the ape is the same medium's "special effects" triumph symbolizing primitive rebellion. With another violation of the world of the text author supplanting the world of the action, these culturally-coded figures become signs pointing at the narrating act:

seguirás su ejemplo y glorificarás la potencia amorosa del simio : poniendo tu pluma al servicio de su desmesura magnífica, entronizando sus prendas con todos los recursos de la insidia verbal : mediante la sutil, emponzoñada subversión de los sacrosantos valores lingüísticos : sacrificando el referente a la verdad del discurso y asumiendo a partir de ella las secuelas de tu delirante desvío : tu maravillosa soledad de corredor de fondo : el desafío insolente al orden real : dejarás que la Parejita se reproduzca entre educados bostezos y conciba y dé a luz un asqueroso niño. [p. 77]

[you will follow his example and glorify the amorous potential of the primate : placing your pen at the service of his magnificent excess, enthroning his endowments with all the devices of verbal chicanery : by means of the subtle, poisoned subversion of the sacrosanct linguistic values : sacrificing the referent to the truth of discourse and assuming with it the consequences of your delirious deviation : your marvelous solitude of a back hallway : the insolent challenge to real order : you will allow the Little Couple to reproduce itself with educated yawns and to conceive and give birth to a loathsome child.]

By transforming the cultural codes into narrative codes, King Kong becomes a sign pointing toward a new rebellious kind of writing, while the Little Couple points to traditional, product-oriented novelistic tenets. In addition, these two characters demonstrate the folly of assuming that art is a direct representation of reality. By juxtaposing the real actress with the fake anthropoid, the text author suggests that artistic reality is never an exact image of external reality—Shirley Temple as projected on the screen is no more a real person that is King Kong. In fact, the Shirley Temple-King Kong combination dramatizes the extent to which art is always separate from and merely an illusion of external reality; it underscores how in art the act of creating the illusion is the only thing that is "real." Thus the metafictional mode of *Juan sin Tierra* serves as a manifesto for a new concept of the relationship between the novel and reality:

la habilidad del relato suplanta la dudosa realidad de los hechos, tu victoria de artista consagra la gesta inútil del militar : descartarás, pues, con desdén la gloria fundada sobre la impostura y decidirás abandonar para siempre tus hueras presunciones de historiador : renunciando a las reglas del juego inane para imponer al lector tu propio y aleatorio modelo en lucha con el clisé común : sin disfrazar en lo futuro la obligada ambigüedad del lenguaje y el ubicuo, infeccioso proceso de enunciación : conmutando desvío rebelde en poder inventivo : recreando tu mundo en la página en blanco. [p. 126]

[the capacity of the fictitious story replaces the questionable reality of facts, your victory as an artist consecrates the futile deeds of the warrior : you will disdainfully sweep aside, then, glory founded on deceit and you will decide to abandon forever your sterile presumptions as a historian : renouncing the rules of the inane game in order to impose on the reader your own and fortuitous model in conflict with the common cliché : without disguising from now on the obligatory ambiguity of language and the ubiquitous, infectious process of enunciation : transforming rebellious deviations into inventive power : recreating your world on the blank page.]

As further binary oppositions are created—Lawrence of Arabia versus the French missionary Père Foucauld, Roman law versus civil anarchy, the traditional realistic mode versus a new self-referential expression—the work frees itself more and more from externally-imposed meaning. This inward turn culminates in the final chapter where the act of narrating completely usurps what is narrated.

In a sense the final chapter of *Juan sin Tierra* is the novel turned inside out; it represents the ultimate violation of the laws of fiction, a transgression of the never-clear line separating metafiction from novelistic theory, fiction from nonfiction:

eliminar del corpus de la obra novelesca los últimos vestigios de teatralidad : transformarla en discurso sin peripecia alguna : dinamitar la inveterada noción del personaje de hueso y carne : substituyendo la *progressio* dramática del relato con un conjunto de agrupaciones textuales movidas por fuerza centrípeta única : núcleo organizador de la propia escritura, plumafuente genésica del proceso textual. [p. 311]

[eliminate from the corpus of the novelistic work the final vestiges of theatricality : transform it into discourse without any turning points : demolish the ingrained notion of characters of flesh and blood : substituting for the dramatic *progressio* of the story a collection of textual juxtapositions motivated by a unique centripetal force : the organizing nucleus of writing itself, engendering fountain pen of the textual process.]

Thus the system of transforming cultural codes into narrative codes is the textual strategy underlying this journey to the core of writing itself. The novel is now exclusively about its own process of coming-into-being. The violation of fictional modes is carried to a new extreme of self-referentiality.

Along with the process of the novel becoming its own referent, and in fact inseparable from it, is the text author's own self-referentiality. By virtue of the second-person familiar narrative voice, he is both the sender and the recipient of his own discourses: "míralos bien : sus rostros te resultarán conocidos" (p. 15) ["look at them closely : their faces will be familiar to you"]. Similar to the phenomenon of a dream in which the dreamer is both the creator and the creation of the dream,[10] the text author is both the source and the object of his own discourses. As he writes, in effect he also reads himself.

In addition to serving as his own text addressee, the text author proposes to become his own progenitor. After first slaughtering the White Dove of Christianity, he sets out to impregnate Yemayá, the pagan goddess of the Cuban slaves' African ancestors: "proseguirás tus incursiones audaces mientras el otro tú guarda dentro la inmediata creación de su cuerpo : inmaterial aún, pero presintiendo ya la vecindad del ser y su futuro, deslumbrante sino" (pp. 56-57) ["you will continue your daring thrusts while the other you waits within for the imminent creation of its body : still formless, but sensing already the proximity of its being and its future, radiating destiny"]. As both his own progenitor and his own progeny, the text author proposes to fuse his own coming-into-being with that of the novel. He is striving to create a new self who will be a new kind of novelist.

To create the new self to serve as the new novelist, the old self must first be destroyed. The second-person familiar narrative voice with its inherent bifurcation facilitates the task of identifying the self that must be sucrificed. It is the self rooted in the cultural history of Spain:

historia desvivida y sobremuerta, epopeya demencial, fúnebre canción de gesta, entonada sobre un fondo mudable do procesiones, sainetes, comedias, corridas de toros, acontecimientos deportivos, alegres zarzuelas, zumbido y furia, bolero de Ravel interminable, gesticulación vana y huera, extendida siglo tras siglo, sin conexiones reales, por pura inercia histórica, hasta el nacimiento del otro, el que tú fueras, en el seno de una atrofiada, extemporánea burguesía, poco más de cuarenta años atrás.[p. 182]

[a lifeless and twice-dead history, a demented epic, a sepulchral *chancon de geste*, recited against a fluctuating background of processions, farces, comedies, bullfights, sporting events, gay operettas, sound and fury, Ravel's interminable bolero, vain and hollow gesticulation, prolonged century after century, without any real connections, out of pure historic inertia, until the birth of the other one, that one that you were, in the bosom of an atrophied, inopportune bourgeois society a little over forty years ago.]

The new novelist, then, must rid himself of the cultural history in which he was born some forty years ago. And once having identified that self, he finally achieves his artistic rebirth, the fruit of his oneiric coitus with the black goddess Yemayá in the initial chapter of the novel: "te has transformado y has transformado el instrumento en que te expresas abandonando en cada hoja de papel blanco jirones y andrajos de tu antigua personalidad hasta alcanzar el estadio actual en que únicamente una fachada nominal y borrosa te identifica" (p. 318) ["you have transformed yourself and you have transformed the instrument with which you express yourself abandoning with each sheet of white paper your old personality until reaching the present state in which only a nominal and blurred facade identifies you"]. He, as well as the novel in which he exists, emerges from a black-white binary opposition. Indeed, his identity as a new novelist is now inseparable from the written text of which he is both speaker and addressee, creator and creation. And whereas he has realized his dual goal of writing a new novel and becoming a new novelist, in the process he has defined forever his reality as the fiction entitled *Juan sin Tierra*.

The fictional reality of which the new novelist is both the creator and the creation ultimately becomes his confinement, his prison-house of language. His quest for a new artistic self is only successful as a quest, as process. It can never be a realization, a product. The only way, therefore, that he can sustain his self-creation is to continue to transform objects from exterior reality into signs pointing toward the creative process. Yet ultimately the system of metonymic associations exhausts itself and the text novelist finds himself threatened by the very system upon which his existence depends. In a final desperate attempt to sustain the process, therefore, he abandons Spanish for another language.

First he writes in a phonetic Spanish: "para seguir a continuasión con el abla ef-fetiba de miyone de pal-lante que diariamente lamplean sin tenén cuenta er código pená impuetto por su mandarinato" (p. 320) ["to continue with the authentic speech of millions of speakers who use it daily without realizing the penal code imposed by its mandarin"]. Soon the phonetic Spanish gives way to a Hispanicized Arabic: "El-Asnam Tanxa Dar-Bida Kuyo trato a pem-mityo er konosimyento Kabal de ty mim-mo i la posyvilidá dep-presal-lo lyberándote de tu hantiryor ympot-tura i, grasias ha la prat-tyca dun lenguage cuep-po, dun belbo beldadelamente echo carne" (p. 320) ["El-Asna Tanxa Dar-Bida whose contact has permitted you a perfect knowledge of yourself and the possibility of expressing it by liberating yourself from your former imposture and, thanks to the practice of a language that has real life to it, of a verb truly made of flesh"]. Next there is Arabic written in Roman transliteration: "qul ya ayuha al-kafirún / la a budu ma ta budún" (p. 320) ["tell them that they do not know

God"]. After a blank page, there is only Arabic script.[11] This final switch in the communication code signals the end of the active communication between fictive author and text-act reader. It also signals the end to the text author's attempts to free language completely from externally-imposed meaning. Language can only be freed from external reality by transforming its cultural codes into narrative codes.

Yet even the final Arabic script cannot erase its cultural codes. The text author has finally been foiled by the very instrument through which he was seeking absolute artistic freedom: language. And so with the end of the linguistic process, exterior reality imposes itself, and the text and the text author are reduced to static black markers on a white page. Thus the novel ends where it began, with a black-white binary opposition—the thread of the seam that unravels the text author's attempt to create his own reality through fiction.

Though the confines of the written text explain the ultimate undoing of the text author's attempt to create a new self, the text-act reader standing beyond these confines is privileged to infinite artistic rebirth. That is to say, although the text author directs his messages to himself and so is his own text reader, the sum total of the intertextual messages fuses into another message directed beyond the boundaries of the written text. This message is directed to the text-act reader. In short, the text-act reader represents the never-clearly-defined point where the work of fiction and the sociohistorical context in which the work was written meet. And since real readers attempt to project themselves into the role of the text-act reader, each new reading and each new reader lead to a different point of contact.[12] As long as there are readers of *Juan sin Tierra* the static black markers will be transformed into the text author's eternal quest for a new novel and a new artistic being. And if each individual reader, like the text author, must ultimately come face to face with the confines of his or her temporal existence, he or she at least is aware of forming a part of a larger system of humanity that, at least one hopes, transcends the confines of our time and space. Each real reader, therefore, represents a link in an infinite chain capable of transforming static letters into dynamic experience, of resurrecting the text author whose dynamic creative process will always end in a static printed artifact.[13] In effect, the real reader represents a final corroboration of art as defined by *Juan sin Tierra:* a dynamic coming-into-being.

The metafictional mode is given a new expression in *Juan sin Tierra*. And although one can detect the imprints of Cervantes, Galdós, Unamuno, Jarnés, and Cunqueiro on Goytisolo's textual strategies, the violations consisting of the world of the text autor first competing with, and then finally supplanting the world of the story represent a more radical metafictional expression than anything we have seen up to this point. Indeed, if the final chapter is read in isolation it almost qualifies as pure novelistic theory—nonfiction. Of course it should not be read in isolation any more than passages from nineteenth-century realistic novels should be isolated from their novelistic context and treated as sociohistorical documentation. Within the artistic process of the novel, the final chapter of *Juan sin Tierra* is a natural culmination of the conflict for predominance between the narrating instance and what is narrated. In the end the creative process triumphs over the created product; the novel becomes its own referent.

Since the novel's projection toward self-referentiality involves the text author's efforts toward self-creation, implicit in the dual processes is the role of the reader in the creative endeavor. In effect the text author of *Juan sin Tierra* is also a reader. Little wonder, therefore, that after the examples of *Recuento, Los verdes de mayo hasta el mar, Novela de Andrés Choz,* and especially *Juan sin Tierra,* all focused on the world of the author and the writing process, the emphasis would finally turn to the world of the reader and the reading process. The next group of self-referential novels to be examined, then, are reader-produced texts.

Chapter Six

Reading-into-Being: *La cólera de Aquiles*

As I proposed in the Introduction and have been arguing throughout this study, there are three basic levels of reading and readers inherent in any fictional text. Each speaker within the world of the story directs his or her discourses to the text addressee, explicit or implicit, embedded within that world. The sum total of the intratextual messages equals another message directed beyond the boundaries of the story to a text-act reader. Finally real readers, in order to apprehend the work's message, project themselves into the role of the text-act reader, a projection that at best can be only partially successful.

Whether speaking of the text reader embedded within the story, or of the text-act reader to whom the story is directed, or of the real reader on whom the whole reading process depends, it is clear that the concept of readers cannot be eliminated from any work of fiction's coming-into-being. It is all but inevitable, therefore, that in its obsession with the creative process, the Spanish self-referential novel would turn its attention to the concept of reading and readers. The resulting reader-produced texts form the second category I am identifying for the Spanish self-referential movement.

The novel that qualifies as the most immediate precursor of the reader-focused metafictional group is Miguel Delibes' *Cinco horas con Mario* (1966) [*Five Hours with Mario*]. In that novel a woman spends the night talking to the corpse of her recently deceased husband and ultimately realizes that she has been talking to herself, that her ostensive criticisms of him are in fact self-confessions. She is her own text addressee. The message directed to the text-act reader, however, seems more concerned with psychosocial aspects of Spain and Spanish women than with fiction's creative process.

The first fiction-in-process novel focused on the world of the reader is Gonzalo Torrente Ballester's *Fragmentos de Apocalipsis* (1977) [*Fragments of the Apocalypse*]. The novel begins with a first-person narrator explaining that he is simultaneously writing a novel and a work diary recording the process of his novelistic efforts. The work diary, therefore, constitutes an attempt to foreground the narrating instance; it represents a violation of the boundary separating the world of the fictive author from the world of the story, since process and product appear on the same narrative level. Yet contrary to what occurs in *Juan sin Tierra*, in which the written text in effect dictates to the text novelist his next step in the writing process, in *Fragmentos de Apocalipsis* the text author uses the diary to analyze and critique what he has written. In short, the diary serves to transform his role from that of writer to that of his own text reader. It forms a circle of nearly absolute artistic self-indulgence.

The pervasive sense of solipsism resulting when an author plays the role of his own reader finally makes the text author/reader of *Fragmentos de Apocalipsis* realize the inherent danger in such a dual role:

Releído, sin embargo, lo que acabo de escribir, no acaba de convencerme. La primera ficción pensada, a poco que se distraiga uno, acabará convirtiéndose en una historia más de James Bond. En cuanto a la segunda, toda vez que el triunfo de la revolución no parece cercano, y que el propio Mao-Tse-Tung le ha dado un par de siglos de plazo, peca indudablemente de idealismo. No sé qué hacer. Tendré que discutirlo con Lénutchka.[1]

[Having reread, nevertheless, what I have just written, I'm not convinced. The first fictitious version conceived, if one becomes the least bit distracted, will end up becoming just another James Bond story. As for the second version, as long as the triumph of the revolution does not seem to be at hand, and Mao-Tse-Tung himself has allowed a couple of centuries before it happens, the story just seems excessively idealistic. I don't know what to do. I will have to discuss it with Lénutchka.]

The text author/reader's decision to involve another reader in his creative process opens a new dimension in the concept of metafiction as a violation of the fictional modes. Not only will this reader transgress the boundary separating one fictional level from another, she will advise the text author in the composition of his novel; she will play not only the role of reader, but that of a reader righting the writer.

Lénutchka's story, according to the text author's explanation, begins before the novel itself. He says that one day he decided to write an erotic story in first-person narrative, but since the only such amorous incidents stored in his memory were from literary sources, he wrote his pseudo-autobiographical narrative based on literary models. In fact, he created a fictitious *persona* for his first-person voice modeled after Don Juan. The text author's fictitious *persona* enjoyed the same success in seduction as his namesake until reaching the end of the list of literary characters for his conquests, at which point the *persona* did the only logical thing: he turned from lover to novelist. By now the original text author's identity was absorbed completely by his fictitious *persona*, to the point that, apparently, it is not the original text author speaking but rather his *persona*. Lénutchka, in the meantime, identifying herself as a Russian professor of literature, had begun a correspondence with the text author about his work, a correspondence that soon evolved into mutual professions of love. The combination of Lénutchka's Russian nationality and the text author's advanced age seemed to eliminate any possibility of consummating their love. Then one day he informed her of his plan to write the very novel which is the subject of the diary: "Un conjunto de palabras, en el que estaré yo mismo, hecho palabra también; con las cartas a la vista, quiero decir, con la advertencia reiterada de que es una ficción verbal, y en modo alguno una historia verdadera ni siquiera verídica" (p. 132) ["A collection of words, in which I myself will be transformed into words also; with all the cards on the table, by that I mean, with the repeated notice that everything is a verbal fiction, and in no sense of the word a true story nor even an authentic one"].

Given Lénutchka's Marxist literary orientation, the text author was surprised when he received a letter in return with a lengthy explanation of the reasons that "la empujaban a pedirme que, ya que otra solución no nos cabía, la metiera también en la novela; es decir, la redujese a mi misma condición de sistema verbal para que, así los dos, en el relato, pudiésemos amarnos" (p. 133) ["prompted her to ask me that, since no other solution was available to us, I include her in the novel also; that is to say, that I reduce her to my own status of a verbal system so that, with the two of us as part of the story, we would be able to love one another"]. This complicated game in which one text novelist is the fictitious creation of another, now progresses to the point where a fictitious character from one narrative level transgresses the boundary of another; Lénutchka steps from the story of the project of writing the novel into the story that is the novel. Fiction begets fiction.

With Lénutchka now a part of the text author's linguistic existence, he can claim credit for creating not only his own lover but a social realist critic determined to counteract his metafictional excesses. Her readings are pitted against his writings. This contradictory situation—a metafictional characacter working against metafiction—gives rise to yet another contradiction. When her criticisms lead the text author to the brink of destroying the manuscript, his love for her stays his hand: "Estuve en aquel momento por destruirlo todo y mandar al diablo el proyecto; pero, si no lo hice fue por no perder a Lénutchka que, con el texto roto, se me iría" (pp. 154-55) ["At that moment I was at the point of destroying everything and saying to hell with the project; but, if I didn't do it, it was so as not to lose Lénutchka who, once the text was torn up, would leave me"].

Torrente's use of a dramatized reader in *Fragmentos de Apocalipsis* underscores in a parodic manner the conflicting yet parallel role of writing and reading in the creative process. Lénutchka is simultaneously an obstacle and a creative impulse; her constant objections to his metafictional mode lead him to the point of destructive exasperation, but she also provides the very reason for the being of the text. Her role in the novel in fact echoes speech act theories and thereby suggests that novels are also speech acts, and the nature of speech acts is determined as much by the receiver as it is by the sender. Indeed, it would not be an exaggeration to say that the receiver is the only justification of the illocutionary speech act. Therefore, when near the end of *Fragmentos de Apocalipsis* the text author, in order to save Lénutchka's reputation from the slanderous comments of another character, removes her from his text—

"Basta con que no piense en ella, con que no vuelva a nombrarla como presente" (p. 376) ["All I have to do is not think about her, not refer to her again"]—he condemns himself to a double failure: "como autor de una novela que jamás escribiré, y como amante de una mujer que no veré jamás. Aceptado esto, ¿qué más me queda?" (p. 376) ["as the author of a novel that I will never write, and as the lover of a woman whom I will never see. Once this is accepted, what is there left for me to do?"]. For the text author, apocalypse is now. Whereas earlier he refrained from destroying the novel out of love for Lénutchka, now the same love has doomed her and the novel. Thus the use of a dramatized reader in *Fragmentos de Apocalipsis* is a textual strategy demonstrating that text writers and text readers are equal and conflicting forces in any novel. They simultaneously work for and against one another in a dynamic process of creation-destruction, a creative-destructive process that is but a dramatized reflection of the linguistic system operating in every literary text as each sign alternately replaces, and is replaced by, another sign. *Fragmentos de Apocalipsis*, by foregrounding the world of the reader, gives new expression to the dynamic essence of language, and thereby to human existence.

Another example of a reader-focused self-referential novel is provided by Javier Tomeo's *El castillo de la carta cifrada (1979)* [*The Castle of the Coded Letter*]. The basic narrator of this novel appears as narrator only in the first sentence of the work: "—No se preocupe, Bautista, y deje de temblar—me dijo aquella mañana el señor Marqués—. Lo que voy a encargarle es fácil"[2] ["—Don't worry, Bautista, and quit trembling—the Marquis told me that morning—. What I am going to have you do is easy"]. After this single indication that what follows is his, Bautista's, account of the Marquis's instructions, the only voice henceforth in the novel is that of the Marquis. In other words, the basic narrator is also the text addressee; he is the implicit sender of the Marquis's recorded speech and the explicit receiver of that speech. The sender-receiver concept is further complicated, however, for whereas the Marquis addresses Bautista, most of his comments concern the reaction he anticipates to a letter he is asking Bautista to deliver. The letter, written in a secret code, is to Don Demetrio López de Costillar. And although the Marquis admits that he himself is not sure of its meaning—"¿Cómo podría explicarle mi carta, si yo mismo no sé muy bien qué es lo que he escrito?" (p. 21) ["How could I explain my letter to you if I myself am not clear as to what I have written?"]—he speculates on the various readings Don Demetrio will give to it. The Marquis, therefore, also plays the dual role of sender and receiver; he is the author and the reader of his own letter. Considering, furthermore, that he himself does not know for sure what he has written, there is a logical illogic to the whole hermeneutic game of guessing the presuppositions that would lead Don Demetrio to what the Marquis defines as "Un universo de interpretaciones" (p. 25) ["A whole universe of interpetations"].

El castillo de la carta cifrada challenges the very distinction we customarily make between authors and readers, between writing and reading. In this novel both speakers actually play the role of addressee. The novel suggests that meaning is not something that originates with the author but rather with the reader. All interpretative reading, therefore, depends on the presuppositions and expectations the reader brings to the text. Indeed, the meaning may well escape the grasp of the author himself, and only by playing the role of his own reader can he hope to approach the meaning of his own utterances. In short, *El castillo de la carta cifrada* violates the laws of fiction by transposing the worlds of the fictive author and of the reader; readers, rather than writers, play the key role in the creative process. Since, furthermore, the role of the reader changes according to the presuppositions and expectations he or she brings to the text, each reading leads to a unique artistic creation.

Yet another reader-focused novel, Juan Marsé's *La muchacha de las bragas de oro* (1978) [*The Girl with the Golden Panties*], presents an old man, a Falangist, dictating his memoirs to his niece. She becomes his critical reader as she constantly challenges his distortions and lies, and in effect usurps his role as writer. As with Delibes' much earlier *Cinco horas con Mario*, however, the message directed to the text-act reader seems more concerned with sociopolitical (and perhaps commercial) concerns than with the artistic creative process. Luis Goytisolo's *La cólera de Aquiles* (1979) [*Achilles' Rage*], on the other hand, seems to define sociopolitical issues in terms of artistic creation-in-process; Luis Goytisolo's novel qualifies as the most radical and profound reader-focused text to emerge in the new wave of Spanish metafiction.

If *Juan sin Tierra* is the paradigm for those self-referential novels foregrounding the world of the fictive author, *La cólera de Aquiles* serves a similar role for those concerned with the world of the reader. For, as the narrator herself states near the end of the novel:

El valor del texto, en lo que a las obras de ficción se refiere, es cosa de la que ya se ocupa—o debiera ocuparse—la crítica literaria. Lo tonto, así pues, de las teorías de la información, es que prescinden de lo que debiera ser lo suyo, que es la lectura. No el texto, sino la lectura del texto. No el contenido en sí del mensaje, sino la lectura en sí de ese mensaje. No la forma en que llegue, sino el impacto que causa. No la bala, sino el balazo. El resto de lo que se diga son especulaciones que valen para el receptor de un télex, y basta.[3]

[As far as works of fiction are concerned, the value of the text is that to which literary criticism is now dedicating itself—or should be dedicating itself. The folly of information theories, therefore, is that they disregard what should be their primary concern, which is the reading: not the text, but rather the reading of the text: not the content itself of the message, but rather the reading itself of that message: not the form in which it may arrive, but rather the impact that it creates: not the bullet, but rather the striking of the bullet. Whatever else may be said is speculation that applies to a telex receiver, and that's it.]

La cólera de Aquiles gives artistic expression to this pronouncement by foregrounding the act of reading. In fact the novel presents writing as merely the graphic response to a reading. And since the response is similar to but always distinct from the text to which it is responding, the relationship reading-writing is based on a structure of differences. With the parallel yet contrasting relationship of reading-writing as the structural axis, therefore, Luis Goytisolo develops his novel around a system of differences that is merely a dramatic reflection of the gulf that always exists between the sign and what the sign attempts to represent.

The concept of writing that is really a reading emerges as the first-person narrator, a lesbian by the name of Matilde Moret, narrates an episode in her past involving herself, her lover Camila, and an Argentine playboy by the name of Roberto who attempted to woo Camila from her. In addition to the "reading" Matilde offers of Camila's and Roberto's motives, she also begins to narrate the content of several letters between the two that she has intercepted. As she narrates this content, however, she is actually reading and interpreting what she is sure is the "real meaning" of each lover's words. In marked contrast to the narrative summary she extends for the letters, she suddenly interrupts her personal story to offer a textual recreation of a novel entitled "El edicto de Milán," ["The Milan Edict"] a work she published several years ago under the pseudonym Claudio Mendoza. Of course the novel represents a fictional reading of her own life. The interpolated novel, which within the framing novel extends over three chapters, consists of three versions of the same basic anecdote. These three "readings," in turn are followed by a reappearance of Matilde as narrator, who then explains and interprets various aspects of "El edicto de Milán." The foregrounding of the reader and the act of reading is further underscored by Matilde's frequent citations of her cousin Raúl's theories on the subject, an example of which appears above. In the case of *La cólera de Aquiles*, then, coming-into-being is reading-into-being.

Luis Goytisolo's initial strategy for directing the focus to reading and the reader is to undermine the speaker's narrative authority. As Matilde narrates the events from the past she employs what Félix Martínez Bonati labels mimetic language, language constituting the "truth" of any fiction—the convention whereby one accepts the existence of Matilde, Camila, and Roberto, for example. Matilde constantly undermines her narrative credibility, however, by interjecting her own views and judgments. Such interjections represent what Martínez Bonati defines as nonmimetic language, language that is subject to the same skeptical scrutiny as any opinionated statement.[4] An example of such a switch from mimetic to nonmimetic language occurs when Matilde notes that Camila finally ended her affair with Roberto, and then adds: "Lo que conmigo hubiera sido posible—una relación profunda—, con ella no lo era. Y eso debía de ser justamente lo que más se temía Camila: que, a la larga, su querido Roberto acabara entendiéndose mejor conmigo que con ella. Celos, en otras palabras" (p. 41) ["What would have been possible with me—a profound relationship—, was not with her. And that must have been exactly what Camila feared most: that, as time went on, her dear Roberto would end up more interested in me than in her. Jealousy, in other words"]. The speculative nature of this utterance changes it from what at first glance might appear to be a narrative statement of fact—fictional fact—to an interpretation, to a reading. The message Matilde directs to her implied text addressee is different from the message the fictive author directs to his implied text-act reader. Her message of uncontestable superiority to Camila becomes a completely opposite message from the perspective of the text-act reader. From such an outside vantage point one might well read Matilde's statement not as an affirmation of superiority but as an expression of inferiority; Camila is not jealous of her, she is jealous of Camila. By engaging in such interpretative speculation, she loses her narrative authority and in effect operates on the level of a reader. As a result, Matilde is automatically pitted against the text-act reader; her reading opposes the reading implicit in the textual strategy of undermining her narrative authority.

The conflict between Matilde's reading and the reading implicit in this textual strategy of discredited authority becomes even more obvious when she turns her attention to the letters she intercepted. She used these letters, she says, to measure the degree of passion between the two lovers, and to be in a position to frustrate its consummation as it intensified. And to complicate her devious scheme, she began to write her own intimate notes in the form of a diary and to leave these notes in a place where she knew Camila would find and read them. Each note was designed to reflect the latest tone she read into Roberto's letters, and so, in her own words, the notes were "respuestas a la respuesta de una respuesta" (p. 42) ["replies to the reply of a reply"]. The repetition of the word "respuesta" underscores the difference between an original text and the texts created by an interpretative reading of the original. The original fades from view as one reading gives rise to another, and this to yet another, in a potentially infinite chain of differences.

Differences in readings are even more dramatic in those instances in which Matilde provides detailed analyses of certain sections from the letters. For example, in one instance apparently some lingering self-doubts compel her to explain a reference to a whale in one of Camila's letters:

Así, aquella frase relativa al cachalote, cuyo alcance, pese a escapárseme de entrada, no dejó por ello de golpearme con dureza, lo confieso, ahora que puedo hacerlo. Tú no sabes lo que es encontrarse con un cachalote en la cama, escribió literalmente Camila en una de esas cartas que dejaba por la casa un tiempo prudencial antes de hacérsela llegar a Roberto. Tardé lo mío, ésta es la verdad, en caer en la cuenta de que, a lo que realmente estaba aludiendo era a mi fogosidad amorosa, una peculiar forma de ferocidad que, para bien o para mal, no puedo menos que reconocer como muy mía. Hubiera quedado mejor poniendo una pantera en lugar de un cachalote, es cierto; pero también más convencional. Aparte de que el oficio de Camila no es precisamente el de escritora. [pp. 308-9]

[Thus that sentence referring to the whale, whose meaning, in spite of escaping me at the time, hit me pretty hard I have to confess, now that I can do it. You don't know what it's like to be in bed with a whale, Camila wrote word for word in one of those letters that she left lying around for a discreet length of time before sending it to Roberto. The truth is it took me quite a while to catch on that she was really alluding to my love-making ardor, a particular form of ferocity that for better or worse I have to recognize as characteristic of me. It would have been better for sure if she had used a panther rather than a whale; but also more conventional. Not to mention that no one ever claimed that Camila has any writing talent.]

While it is impossible to say that Matilde's interpretation of the reference is irrefutably wrong, it seems forced at the very least. Even she has to admit that a whale is not the most felicitous image to connote passion. In fact, a more common connotation for a whale is bulk, and such a connotation suggests the need to reread some of Matilde's earlier supposedly mimetic utterances when she referred to her own "perfecta forma física" (p. 31) ["perfect figure"] or described herself as "alta, esbelta, elegante" (p. 60) ["tall, slim, elegant"]. Whether a question of Matilde's mistaken self-image, her attempt to deceive her text addressee, Camila's spitefulness, or any number of other possibilities, the convention attributing uncontestable truth to certain utterances in fiction is now challenged. What initially was read as a statement of fact now must be reread as an opinion subject to multiple interpretations. And if the implication is followed to its next logical step, that all writing is but the graphic expression of a reading of what preceded it, it becomes clear that infallible authority in all fiction is but an illusion, an arbitrary convention. With this in view, Matilde's "unreliability" as a narrator (in the Wayne Booth sense of the word) functions as a sign suggesting that the very concept of reliability is in fact a contradiction inherent in language, which seems to indicate presence when in fact it marks absence. This structure of difference essential to language itself is dramatized by the conflict between Matilde's readings and the responses implicitly elicited by such readings.

Even when Matilde does not intrude as a reader, a structure of differences imposes itself. As the interpolated novel, "El edicto de Milán," unfolds in chapters four, five, and six, for example, Matilde's only claim to existence is as the implied author of it. Furthermore, since she published the novel under the pseudonym Claudio Mendoza, she is removed yet another step. In fact, in chapter four, where the interpolated novel begins, the whole notion of an implied author is limited to the shifting point of focalization from which the action is presented. As the story begins Lucía is alone in the Paris train station just after her fiancé Luis has departed for Spain to work for the Communists against the dictatorship. As she leaves the station the point of focalization shifts subtly between an inside and an outside view:

La estación súbitamente inanimada y silenciosa no bien el tren hubo partido. Las aceras resbaladizas que, como en un sueño, se alargaban y alargaban según ella iba avanzando, el pelo suelto, las manos en los bolsillos de la gabardina, el olor a llovizna como un aliento que empaña los cristales, y como la mirada de un loco el brillo gris del pavimento.[pp. 97-98]

[The station suddenly lifeless and silent no sooner had the train departed. The slippery sidewalks that, as if in a dream, stretched on and on the more she advanced, her hair blowing in the wind, her hands in the pockets of her jacket, the smell of mist like a breath that frosts over a window pane, and the gray glow of the payment like the gaze of a madman.]

The shifting point of focalization, which initially offers her view of the station and of the dreamlike extension of the sidewalk and then moves outside to describe her physically, and finally back inside as she sees and feels the mist in the air, and on the pavement, implies the presence of a manipulating hand behind it. Yet the images of loneliness tend to all but erase the awareness of an implied author and to encourage identification with the protagonist, with her illusory reality. The artifices and conventions of fiction are backgrounded, overpowered by the illusions they create. As a result, Lucía and her world seem real. This illusion of reality prevails throughout the anecdote as Lucía feels abandoned by Luis and suspects him of being involved with a female political colleague in Spain. Her trip to Sète to meet him for a weekend only intensifies her conviction that he now loves someone else. On her return to Paris she is merely an observer of the shifting sexual entanglements of her university friends until finally succumbing to a one-night affair with a Cuban mulatto named Camilo. The chapter ends with her arrival at Barcelona, where she is to marry Javier, another of her university friends but one singled out for always conducting himself as a real gentleman.

Chapter five repeats the basic anecdote of chapter four, but with significant differences:

Dos cosas, por libre que una sea, hay que tener muy claras: lo que se puede y lo que no se puede hacer, dijo Lucía. Algo que Gina era capaz de entender perfectamente, pese a los embrollos morales que le creaba su desdichada propensión a caer siempre en los brazos de tíos mitad chorizos, mitad revolucionarios, dispuestos a explotar a fondo su mala conciencia de niña bien milanesa. Algo, en cambio, que era del todo inútil pretender explicar a Charlotte, para quien esta clase de consideraciones había que situarlas—no menos aceptables, pero tampoco de mayor validez—en un mismo plano, por ejemplo, que un proyecto de viaje en moto al Japón o un caso de vocación religiosa. Que Lucía se negara, sin ir más lejos, a salir con alguien que tuviese pareja, a robar el hombre a nadie, casados o no casados, eso era lo de menos. Con gente como Camilo, sí: igualmente libres ambos, de igual a igual; Lucía, en definitiva, no era precisamente una estrecha. Pero eso de romper la unidad de una pareja, con el resultado seguro de que el sufrimiento de alguien estaba en juego, lo dejaba para personas tipo Marina o Irenita, La Princesa Roja. [p. 139]

[No matter how free a girl may be, she has to keep two things in mind: what she can and cannot get away with, Lucía said. Something that Gina was perfectly capable of understanding, in spite of moral entanglements that were created for her by her unfortunate propensity to always fall into the arms of guys who were part pigs, part revolutionaries, ready to exploit to the limit her guilty conscience as a nice girl from Milan. Something, on the other hand, that was totally useless to try to explain to Charlotte, for whom this type of consideration had to be placed—no less acceptable, but no more valid either—on the same level, for example, as the plans for a motorcycle trip to Japan or the decision to enter a convent. The fact that Lucía would refuse, at least, to go out with someone who had a partner, to rob a man from anyone, married or not, was no big deal. With guys like Camilo, sure: both equally free, on even terms; indeed, Lucía was not exactly a blushing virgin. But the business of breaking up a couple, with the certainty that someone's suffering was a part of the game, she left that for persons like Marina or little Irena, the Red Princess.]

Unlike the beginning of the interpolated novel offered in the previous chapter, where the view stresses images conveying the sensation of loneliness and vulnerability, in this second version of her story the indirect recorded speech places the emphasis on mental processes. These processes, rather than projecting an image of vulnerability, characterize her as a street-wise woman whose brazen image is tempered only by her particular sense of honor. Yet even this sense of honor is undermined by the sarcasm with which she speaks of her friends, and by the suggestion that the underlying motive of the sarcasm is self-pity (Irena, the "Princesa Roja," is the woman she suspects of having stolen Luis's affections). Such an introduction to the "new" Lucía is followed directly by details of her extended relationship with Camilo (as opposed to the single affair narrated in the previous chapter), a relationship she finally terminates after tiring of his unorthodox sexual proclivities. Furthermore, in this chapter Lucía has affairs with several men in addition to Camilo, including one in the bathroom with the conductor of the train she takes to visit Luis in Sète. The chapter ends, however, with her arrival once again in Barcelona where she is to marry the wealthy and ingenuous Javier. As the protagonist becomes less appealing and contradictions arise between the first and second versions of her story, one begins to detect the presence of Matilde as the functional creator hiding behind her creation.

The conclusion of "El edicto de Milán" is offered in chapter six, yet it is nothing more than a third version of Lucía's basic story:

En definitiva, una tiene que hacer lo que le gusta hacer, y la única forma de saber qué es exactamente lo que a una le gusta hacer es probarlo todo primero. Son cosas sobre las que resulta imposible pronunciarse hasta que las has hecho, hasta que las has probado. Y si das un no de antemano, quiere decir, no ya que tienes prejuicios, sino, que inconscientemente, estás temiendo el sí, su atracción sobre ti. Para la gente, piensen como piensen, hay siempre una norma moral a la que debes adecuar tu conducta. Yo, en cambio, pienso que es la moral la que se debe acomodar a ti, a tus gustos, a tu manera de ser. [p. 171]

[Indeed, one has to do what one likes to do, and the only way of knowing exactly what one likes to do is to try everything once. There are things that are impossible to pass judgment on until you have done them, until you have tried them. And if you say no beforehand, it means, not only do you have prejudices, but subconsciously you are afraid to say yes, you are afraid of their attraction for you. No matter what people may think, for them there is always a moral norm to which you should adjust your conduct. On the other hand I believe that morality should accommodate itself to you, to your preferences, to your personality.]

With this third "reading" of Lucía, one begins to detect more clearly the presence of Matilde as the implied author. Such a presence emerges first with the totally self-indulgent, amoral, attitude of Lucía. It is reinforced later in the anecdote when Lucía confesses to a lesbian affair with Charlotte and a *ménage á trois* episode involving another female friend and a man characterized in the earlier versions by his renowned sadomasochistic tendencies. In addition to these personality echoes of Matilde's own life, the quoted passage offers the first example of a first-person narrative voice ("Yo, en cambio, pienso"). Since the first-person narration is not sustained, it functions as a violation of the embedded novel's narrative voice; it makes explicit the presence of the fictional author Matilde. So as the second and third versions of Lucía create more distance between the text reader and the protagonist, the artifices and conventions of fiction edge ever so slowly to the foreground. Each reading with variations constitutes an artifice in itself, and also underscores the structure of differences on which the whole novel is constructed.

With the end of the interpolated novel, Matilde reclaims her role as narrator, and in an even more pronounced manner, that of reader. Not only does she continue to offer self-readings along with readings of other intercepted letters, she now directs a major portion of her efforts to commenting on "El edicto de Milán," to correcting what she considers the misreading of it by the very person to whom she was addressing it, her cousin Raúl. Not only is she reading her own novel, she is also "correcting" someone else's reading of it.

In her role as reader of Lucía's fictitious story, moreover, Matilde offers another challenge to the concept of "suspension of disbelief." Whereas before Lucía, especially in the first version, projected an illusion of reality, of being a real person, now Matilde completely unmasks that illusion with her commentary; she dramatically reduces Lucía to a fiction by explaining the strategies underlying the illusion of reality. But then suddenly Matilde lays bare the illusion of her own reality as she begins to boast of her textual strategies concerning the work's final paragraph:

> La ambigüedad de tal párrafo, como la de tantos otros, es, por supuesto, totalmente premeditada. Vamos, una broma en forma de trampa que tiendo al crítico avezado para que, recogiendo algunos cabos que dejo sueltos con malignidad calculada, analizando algunos lapsus, alguna que otra incoherencia, pueda llegar a la sagaz conclusión de que Claudio Mendoza es una mujer y, por añadidura, lesbiana. De ahí que cualquier hipotético lector de las presentes líneas pueda concluir a su vez, no menos sagazmente y en virtud del mismo juego de compensaciones, en que mi nombre, Matilde Moret, encubre un varón; cosa, por otra parte, acaso más cierta de lo que a primera vista pueda suponerse. [pp. 201- 2]

> [The ambiguity of such a paragraph, like that of so many others, is, of course, totally premeditated. Okay, a joke in the form of a trap that I lay out for the astute critic so that he, by recollecting some loose ends I leave lying about with calculated malice, by analyzing some lapses, a few inconsistencies, may arrive at the clever conclusion that Claudio Mendoza is a woman and, moreover, a lesbian. Following the same line of reasoning any hypothetical reader of the present lines may conclude on his part, no less cleverly and by virtue of the same set of logic, that my name, Matilde Moret, disguises a male; something, on the other hand, perhaps truer than one may imagine at first glance.]

When the narrator says that "mi nombre, Matilde Moret, encubre un varón," she shatters completely the convention of "suspension of disbelief." In effect this discourse is now directed to the text-act reader. Matilde is not speaking to a text addressee embedded within the world of the story; the fictive author is speaking through her to the text-act reader stationed outside that world. And since the communication act now extends beyond the boundaries of the fictitious world, suddenly the *persona* of Luis Goytisolo emerges as the ultimate manipulating hand behind this game of gender and authorship. The real reader identifying with the text-act reader, therefore, can now reconstruct the game in which Luis Goytisolo, or his *persona*, creates a fictitious woman, Matilde, who pretends to create a fictitious man, Claudio, who pretends to create on his part a fictitious character, Lucía.

But such a reconstruction from outside the boundary of the fictitious world does not adequately explain the novel. *La cólera de Aquiles* is not only a game exposed as merely a game, but also an aesthetic experience based on illusion. In terms of the aesthetic experience Lucía is the most "real" of all the characters in the novel. With an eye turned to the artifices and conventions of the game, however, she is not only fictitious but a fiction three times removed. In effect this laying bare of the game places the illusion under erasure—crossed out, as Derrida, following Heidegger's lead, graphically demonstrates the concept. Yet since it is merely under erasure, the illusion is still visible, the aesthetic experience still exists. By violating the boundary separating text speaker and addressee from fictive author and text-act reader, and thereby placing the illusion under erasure, another dimension of fiction's inherent structure of differences surfaces: its function as a sign signaling the absence rather than the presence of reality. And if on the one hand the illusion is obviously inadquate and therefore must be crossed out, on the other hand it is a necessary complement of, yet never a substitute for, reality. In fact, the recognition of fiction as a sign of absence can also be seen as directly related to the concept of reading: every work of fiction is merely the response to another work, another link in a chain of differences created by a futile but dynamic search for the ultimate fusion of language and reality, of art and existence.

Such a search finally leads Matilde to a rereading of a work predating written literature, the story of Achilles. She feels his story may serve as a point of reference for defining her own sense of anguish. Achilles's mother, Matilde recalls, took him from under Chiron's tutelage and, dressing him like a girl, placed him in a sort of convent to hide him from his enemies. Matilde reads this episode as an example of a person's natural inclinations being diverted by an outside force; therefore Achilles is a symbol for her of "aquel que no ha logrado superar la creencia de haber sido víctima, en sus primeros años, de la traición y el abandono, de haber sido sometido a las reglas de un mundo que no era el suyo, constreñido a simular una manera de ser que nada tiene en común con la que le es propia" (p. 274) ["someone who has not managed to recover from the feeling of having been a victim in his early years of betrayal and abandonment, of having been subjected to the rules of a world that was not his own, obliged to conduct himself in a manner that has nothing to do with his own personality"]. Not only is she postulating a unique reading of the Achilles story, but the referent for the reading is not the written text; the referent is a painting by Poussin entitled "La cólera de Aquiles" that she saw in the Louvre. Yet, as Matilde confesses near the end of the novel, she has never been able to find this painting again in the museum, nor even in the catalogue of Poussin's complete works. She finally admits that perhaps the painting was by someone else, or that it never existed. The source from which Matilde arrived at her new reading transcends her own consciousness. In fact, the attempts on her part to arrive at a single source diminish the fictional creation—as is demonstrated by her efforts to identify and explain the referents for the characters in "El edicto de Milán." In the case of the painting, the problem of its identity provides a glimpse into the infinite network of texts inherent in the very concept of literary source.

The idea of a source as an infinite network of texts, and of the discovery that there is a chain of common human experiences extending far beyond any individual's capacity for recognizing what forces are influencing his or her readings, allows Matilde to see a link between Achilles and her own addressee: "Yo escribo para quien sea consciente de que, en definitiva, en mayor o menor grado, todos hemos sido víctimas de la dicotomía a la que estoy refiriéndome, de que a todos se nos ha robado algo de nosotros mismos" (p. 274)["I am writing for someone who is conscious that beyond any doubt, to a greater or lesser degree, we have all been victims of the dichotomy to which I am referring, that we have all been robbed of some part of ourselves"]. Matilde may be suggesting that although no one can define this something that has been taken from all of us, everyone should sense the imprint of this something on any work of fiction, not just on hers. As a result of its amorphous outline, however, each reader will interpret this something distinctly. That is, each reader creates his or her own text while reading, a text whose identity will always be defined by the difference between it and the previous one. Thus readings inspire other readings in an infinite process leading inexorably away from the very source they are designed to reach.

La cólera de Aquiles demonstrates that there are as many texts of the novel as there are readers who attempt to close the gap between themselves and the implicit text-act reader. Although this gap exists for every fictional work, its existence is exaggerated by Luis Goytisolo's textual strategy in this novel of creating multiple text addressees (Matilde directs her replies to the letters to Camila, her novel "El edicto de Milán" to Raúl, and her comments on the letters, the novel, and everything else to a secret recipient). The message sent to each of these text addressees, moreover, is different from that directed to the text-act reader, a text-act reader with whom each real reader attempts to identify and thereby apprehend the work's composite message. Since the ability to achieve such an identification can never be totally successful, "the message" of the novel is always deferred to an infinite future of yet another reading. If the self-referential novels represented by *Juan sin Tierra* seem to write themselves into existence, those represented by *La cólera de Aquiles* may be said to read themselves into existence. Whereas the writer-focused group supplants the story with the process of writing, the reader-focused novels transpose fictive author and reader. Readers create texts. All writing, therefore, is defined as merely the graphic expression of a reading. *La cólera de Aquiles*, as the paradigm of the reader-produced group, might best be described as the reading of a reading of a reading.[5] In this group of novels, then, the respective worlds of the fictive author and of the story are not merely violated but literally ingested by the world of the reader.

In the more radical expression of the self-referential novel examined in the next chapter, there is an attempt to reduce the triad of the fictional mode to a single all-assimilating cell. As if in response not only to the reader-dominated but also to the writer-dominated texts, the third category of self-referential novels effaces both fictive author and reader. The written fictional mode emerges only at the end of the characters' oral discoursing.

Chapter Seven

Product Preceding Process: *El cuarto de atrás*

In the two categories previously proposed for the Spanish self-referential novel the narrating instance is foregrounded. Since the narrating instance involves both a sender and a receiver, the first group is identified as author-focused and the second as reader-focused. The first group examines the process of creating the written work through the act of writing, and the second group explores the same process through the act of reading. In either case the emphasis is shifted from the product (story) to the process (act of narrating). In the third group the emphasis is directed back to the story, but in such a way that it seems that the product (story) precedes the process (act of narrating).

Essential to the illusion that process and product are transposed is a focus on the pre-writing stage of novelistic creation. That is to say, we are offered the illusion that the novel does not yet exist, that the characters, who in all my examples are fictitious authors, are laying the groundwork for what will become the written work. Their discourse, therefore, is made to appear oral. When and if they manage to transform this oral discourse into writing, they will have created a work of fiction, complete with the world of the fictive author and the world of the text-act reader. In this final category demonstrating different methods for violating the laws of fiction, then, the fictional mode itself must be created.

Perhaps Juan Goytisolo was the first novelist to signal the nature of my third category of self-referential novels when, in an interview focused on his recently published *Juan sin Tierra*, he said to Julián Ríos: "Si vuelvo a escribir será tal vez a partir de un nuevo sincretismo creador—como llamaba Broch al arte de Joyce o de Picasso—buscando el medio de superar el esquema historia/

discurso de Benveniste"[1] ["If I write again perhaps it will be based on a new creative syncretism—as Broch called the art of Joyce or Picasso—a search for a means of surpassing Benveniste's story/discourse paradigm"]. In his subsequent novel *Makbara* (1980), Goytisolo attempts to bridge this gap between product (story) and process (discourse) by creating a speaker who is a teller of tales, a minstrel who assumes the role of all the characters he invents. Near the end of the novel the speaker attempts to define what he sees as a new oral fictional mode:

liberación del discurso, de todos los discursos opuestos a la normalidad dominante . . . posibilidad de contar, mentir, fabular, verter lo que se guarda en el cerebro y el vientre, el corazón, vagina, testículos : hablar y hablar a borbollones, durante horas y horas : vomitar sueños, palabras, historias hasta quedarse vacío : literatura al alcance de analfabetos, mujeres, simples, chiflados : de cuantos se han visto tradicionalmente privados de la facultad de expresar fantasías y cuitas : condenados a callar, obedecer, ocultarse, comunicar por murmullos y signos : al amparo de la oficiosa neutralidad del lugar : de la impunidad del juglar que zahiere tras la máscara falaz de la risa : oradores sin púlpito ni tribuna ni atril : poseídos de súbito frenesí : charlatanes, embaucadores, locuaces, todos cuentistas.[2]

[freedom of the discourse, of all the discourses opposed to the dominating normal state of things . . . the possibility of telling, of lying, of fabulating, of spilling out what is guarded in the brain and the gut, the heart, the vagina, the testicles : speaking and speaking in a flood, for hours on end : vomiting dreams, words, stories until being empty : literature accessible to the illiterate, to women, to retarded people, to fools : to all who have traditionally been deprived of the facility to express fantasies and troubles : condemned to remain silent, to obey, to hide, to communicate by means of murmurs and signs : aided by the complacent neutrality of the setting : by the impunity of the minstrel who criticizes behind the false mask of laughter : orators without benefit of a pulpit or tribunal or podium : suddenly possessed with a frenzy : charlatans, tricksters, chatterboxes, all story tellers.]

Thus Goytisolo attempts to fabricate an illusion that we are not reading words but rather listening to oral speech. We have circled back to the oral tradition where everyone who wishes can be a novelist. In such an oral mode there is no implied author hidden behind the speaker and no text-act reader standing beyond the world of the listeners. The narrating act occurs within the world of the story. In short, literature has surpassed the constraints of the written word, and in so doing violates the very laws of fiction. Rather than process (discourse) creating a product (story), the two seem to fuse. The act of discoursing *is* the story of *Makbara*,[3] or so Goytisolo's textual strategies would have us believe. Yet even more daring than Juan's attack on the modes of fiction is that offered by his brother Luis in one of his more recent novels.

In *Teoría del conocimiento* (1982) *[Theory of Knowledge]* Luis Goytisolo's final installment to the tetralogy *Antagonía*, the story also seems to occur before the act of writing the story. By means of three successive speakers there is a general movement from written to oral discourse, a movement that also leads from the planning stage toward the actual creation of a novel. Initially there are merely entries of a diary, followed by notes for a novel recorded on a cassette, and finally the voice of a man dictating the novel into a tape recorder. Although there does seem to be a progression toward the completed work, that work in its written form remains an unfulfilled project of the future as the process leads away from, rather than toward, the written word.

The textual strategy behind the illusion that fiction precedes itself, that rather than a novel we are offered the preliminary stages in creation of the novel, centers on the three speakers. Each speaker is an aspiring author, and in a circular process each contributes to the others' creative efforts.

The circular process begins with Carlos writing his diary. Among his preoccupations is a woman living across from him whom he observes regularly from his window. As he writes he wonders exactly what emotion was aroused in him when he first saw her, and especially when he first learned that her name was Aurea:

Responder a esta cuestión no es más fácil que responder a la pregunta de por qué escribo, de por qué estoy ahora redactando estas líneas. Y conste que no me refiero al hecho de que lo que estoy escribiendo sea un diario, al problema de por qué una persona escribe su diario, sino al hecho de escribir en sí . . . el fenómeno de la escritura a toda contingencia ajena a la conciencia de estar siendo lo que realmente es que posee el escritor en el acto de proyectarse hacia el exterior por medio de su obra, de una obra que—él lo sabe bien—escapa al dominio de su conciencia en la medida en que se objetiviza, en la medida en que se convierte en réplica antagónica de si mismo.[4]

[To respond to that question is no easier than responding to the question of why I am writing, of why I am transcribing these lines. And let it be clear that I am not referring to the fact that what I am writing happens to be a diary, to the problem of why a person writes a diary, but to the fact of writing itself . . . the phenomenon of writing removed from every contingency other than the consciousness that the writer possesses of being what he really is in the act of projecting himself toward the exterior by means of his work, of a work that—he knows very well—escapes the control of his consciousness to the degree that it becomes objectified, to the degree to which it is transformed into an opposing replica of himself.]

Clearly for Carlos the act of writing is an existential affirmation of his being, while the written product opposes that being. Apparently, therefore, he prefers to write a diary in which he muses about writing a novel rather than to write the novel itself. He feels the need to keep the process—his means of self-affirmation—separate from the product. In fact, his dream is "encontrarme un buen día con un libro mío en los escaparates, inesperado como uno de esos hongos que brotan, se diría, de la noche a la mañana; que la presencia de mi libro y mi aparición como escritor coincidan hasta superponerse, hasta hacer ociosa cualquier clase de explicación o conjetura" (p. 63) ["one fine day just to run into a book of mine in a store window, as unexpected as one of these mushrooms that just sprout forth, as they say, overnight; I want the presence of my book and my emergence as a writer to coincide to the point of occurring one on top of the other, to the point of rendering useless any kind of explanation or conjecture"]. The written work threatens to poison its creator. The antidote is to sustain the process of writing.

Ricardo, the second author within the work, also writes. But after writing the notes from which he one day intends to create a novel, he records them. His solution to the threat of the written work is to transform the writing into oral discourse. For him, then, writing is a preliminary but necessary step in the creative process: "Escribir como pensar perfeccionando, como forma de dar agudeza a la idea, de articularla con otras y organizar el conjunto. La palabra escrita no será ni más ni menos cierta que la palabra pensada por el mero hecho de haberse objetivado; lo que sí ganará, en cuanto expresión, es coherencia respecto a sí misma" (p. 77) ["Writing as a means of perfecting the thought process, a form of sharpening the idea, of articulating it with others and organizing the whole. The written word will not be any more or less certain than the unwritten word merely because it has been objectified; what it will gain, as far as expression is concerned, is coherence in respect to itself"]. Perhaps because Ricardo is an architect by profession, he uses writing as a blueprint for his artistic construction. He is a planner, not a builder. In fact, his ideal is a creation that will not be a novel, but rather a pre-novel:

> Pues bien: imaginemos una obra así, en la que, de cada una de sus partes surjan otras que a su vez generen otras y otras, en un despliegue más y más vasto. Esta fue mi idea primitiva de la obra en proyecto, una idea que no tardó en completarse y definirse hasta quedar concretada en lo que es ahora, el proyecto de una obra compuesta por diversos libros . . . aproximarse . . . al proceso de gestación de la obra, las notas tomadas, los escritos previos, a ser posible en el contexto en que fueron escritos. [p. 218]

[Okay: let's imagine such a work, in which, from each of its components emerge others that in turn generate still others, in an unfolding more and more vast. This was my original idea for the projected work, an idea that did not take long in becoming finalized and defined until ending up in the concrete form of what is now a project composed of diverse books . . . approach . . . the process of gestation of the work, the notes jotted down, the preliminary drafts, if at all possible within the context in which they were written.]

Obviously the work he is defining is a mirror of the very work of which he is a part. And whereas Carlos wants to sustain the process of writing and dreams of seeing the product sprout forth one day as some kind of phenomenon of nature, Ricardo proposes to eliminate the product. Ricardo is striving for a perpetual "obra en proyecto."

The final speaker in the novel, a nameless old man, although also an aspiring novelist, eschews writing completely. He is dictating his novel into a tape recorder, and his typist will then transpose the dictation into written form. The old man, familiar with the works of his two predecessors, has taken steps to assure that he will receive exclusive recognition for his creation:

> Este es precisamente el gran riesgo: la obra apócrifa, la falsa atribución de una obra a un autor, sea premeditadamente, por insaciable vanidad del que usurpa, sea por mera confusón interpretativa, por deducción errónea. Veamos si no cuál es la situación y qué es lo que se halla en juego: tenemos el diario del joven Carlos, una copia mecanografiada que, a falta de datos más explícitos acerca de su desdichado autor, cualquier futuro estudioso puede llegar a pensar que se trata de una obra de ficción escrita por Ricardo Echave, dada la seguridad con que éste se refiere a determinados aspectos de su contenido. Tenemos también lo que yo llamo el Libro de Ricardo, esto es, la grabación del contenido de sus notas realizada por él mismo. Y están, finalmente, mis cintas, estas cintas que Carlos convierte cada noche en transcripción mecanografiada, justo el procedimiento inverso al seguido por Ricardo Echave. Una situación, sobra decirlo, que convierte a Carlos en depositario único de todos esos materiales. Y Carlos tiene mi confianza, ya que su elección como transcriptor y despositario se debe a lo que vi en el iris de sus ojos tanto acerca de su vida cuanto acerca de su carácter, pasivo por excelencia, falto de imaginación, de cualidades creadoras, el transcriptor ideal, en suma. [pp. 310-11]

[This is precisely the great risk: the apocryphal work, the false crediting of a work to an author, whether it is a case of premeditation, of insatiable vanity of the plagiarizer, of mere interpretative confusion, of an erroneous deduction. Let's see what the situation is, and what the game is all about: we have young Carlos's diary, a recorded copy of which, were it not for explicit data concerning its unfortunate author, some future scholar might well arrive at the erroneous conclusion that it is a fictional work written by Ricardo Echave, in view of the certainty with which the latter refers to certain aspects of its content. We also have what I call Ricardo's Book, that is to say, the tapings he made himself of the content of his notes. And finally, here we have my tapes, these tapes that Carlos each night converts to typewritten script, just the inverse process to that followed by Ricardo Echave. A situation, it goes without saying, that makes Carlos the sole depository of all those materials. And Carlos has my confidence, since his selection as transcriber and depository is a result of what I saw in the iris of his eyes concerning not only his life but his character, exemplary passivity, lack of imagination and creative qualities, in short, the ideal transcriber.]

The speaker's preoccupation with being recognized as the true creator of his novel is ironic on several levels. First of all, apparently he himself has plagiarized from young Carlos and Ricardo, a plagiarism implicit in his explanation that his typist will be the sole depository of *all* the materials. In addition, the speaker's pretentions of being the final authentic voice in the work are dramatically undermined by the existence of not one, but two title pages—the first listing Luis Goytisolo and the second listing Raúl Ferrer Gaminde as the author of the novel. Not only is he unable to erase the imprint of his predecessors from his work, but he is also a mere pawn in a dispute over authorship between the fictive and the real author. And since the whole process in which he aspires to be at the top of the authorial hierarchy actually begins and ends with Carlos (the typist is the father of the young Carlos writing his diary), the very concept of authorship is reduced to a circle of intratextual borrowing, of one author mirroring another.

A mirror perhaps best conveys the narrative process of *Teoría del conocimiento*. The text functions as a series of mirrors, with the image in each mirror reflecting the reverse side of the image preceding it. Thus oral becomes written discourse, and written becomes oral discourse. In such a text the process of discourse never ends as a static artifact. In short, the novel appears to move toward its own creation but without ever becoming the created product. The fictional mode, it seems, remains a potential yet to be realized.[5]

Carmen Martín Gaite's *El cuarto de atrás* (1978) [*The Back Room* in the English version] offers the most dramatic example of the Spanish self-referential novel's illusion that the story precedes the act of writing the story. In fact, in this story-focused novel the protagonist, by virtue of her discourses with a stranger and with her own past, creates the fictional mode of the novel; only on the last page of the novel does the novel seem to become a novel.

The anecdote involves a first-person narrator who falls asleep one evening only to be awakened by a stranger claiming to have arrived for his appointment to interview her, an appointment she does not remember having made. Whether the stranger is "real" or a part of her dream is never clear as he begins to quiz her about the books she has published and about her current literary projects. As they talk her thoughts are constantly interrupted by flashbacks to personal incidents in her life, and to lines from pop songs, pulp magazines, sentimental novels, classroom texts, literary classics, etc., all a chaotic but integral part of her sociocultural development. At one point the stranger gestures at a small stack of typewritten pages on a table and asks if they are a part of one of her current projects. She assures him they are not, and in fact insists she has no idea of their origin or content. Even an interrupting phone call in which the protagonist talks with someone claiming to be the interviewer's lover, a woman who just may be a character from one of the protagonist's novels, fails to alter the pattern of dialogue in the present triggering fragments from the past. And as the process continues, the two notice that the stack of pages off in the corner seems to be growing. Finally the wind scatters the pages, and as the stranger begins to place them back in order, she falls asleep. She is awakened by the return of her daughter from a late date, and although the protagonist is alone, there are two glasses on a tray. She tells her daughter that she cannot explain the two glasses for she spent the evening alone. As the protagonist finally reaches to turn out the light, she notices that the stack of papers is on her nighttable and now numbers one hundred and eighty-two pages. The title is, "El cuarto de atrás," and the first paragraph she reads is the same as the first paragraph with which the novel began.

The image of the written manuscript of the novel appearing within the novel itself represents an aesthetic expression of the distinction Barthes, for example, has made between the work and the text. The work is the static black markers on the page, the artifact, the object one holds in one's hands; the text, on the other hand, is held only in language itself, it exists only as discourse.[6] When, therefore, the protagonist picks up the manuscript entitled, "El cuarto de atrás," it appears as the product of the discoursing in which she has been involved up to that moment. By the same token when we read the final words narrating her act of picking up the manuscript, we suddenly become aware of the novel we hold in our hands, and see it now as a mere artifact, the product of the discoursing in which we have been aesthetically participating. The text then emerges, independent as it were, of the written word. As a result, the role we play as the text-act reader in this novel is really not that of reader at all, but rather that of a participant in discourse. Underlying such an aesthetic experience are textual strategies involving the protagonist-narrator's process of dramatizing her addressee, of forsaking historical narration, and of espousing the fantastic mode. When at the end of such a process the artifact entitled "El cuarto de atrás" emerges, the protagonist can lay claim to having created her own narrator, reader, and story, all three of which she holds in her hands. Such is the nature of Carmen Martín Gaite's contribution to the contemporary Spanish novel's assault on the fictional modes.

The transformation of the text addressee from a mere implicature of fictional discourse to a dramatized character represents a key strategy for directing the focus to the world of the characters and action in *El cuarto de atrás*. As the novel begins the protagonist-narrator is alone in her house and her narrating act is directed to an implied text addressee—a conventional narrative situation. Just before falling asleep, however, she invokes the appearance of an interlocutor: "las estrellas se precipitan y aún tengo tiempo de decir 'quiero verte, quiero verte', con los ojos cerrados; no sé a quien se lo digo"[7] ["the stars are tumbling down and I still have time to say 'I want to see you, I want to see you,' with my eyes closed; I don't know to whom I am saying it"]. In apparent answer to her plea, the next chapter opens with the telephone ringing and the voice of a man announcing that he is there for the interview. Whether dream or fictional reality, the narrator has given an identity to, if not actually created,[8] her text addressee; furthermore, she has bestowed upon him the capacity to respond. Indeed, he responds not only to the comments she directs toward him but to her unspoken thought processes. In short, rather than a narrator narrating, from the second chapter on she becomes a fictional character talking with another fictional character.

The subject of the conversation between the protagonist and the stranger is basically the same one she was directing to her implied recipient in the first chapter: whether to write a historical account or a fictional one of the Franco years. The project to write a factual account in the form of memoirs occurred to the protagonist the day she watched the dictator's funeral on television. Since that day she has been collecting data to facilitate the task. Rather than an assistance, however, the data have become an obstacle: "¡Qué aglomeración de letreros, de fotografías, de cachivaches, de libros . . .!; libros que, para enredar más la cosa, guardan dentro fechas, papelitos, telegramas, dibujos, texto sobre texto" (p. 16) ["What an accumulation of labels, photographs, souvenirs, books . . .!; books that, to complicate the whole thing even more, have within their covers dates, scraps of paper, telegrams, drawings, one text on top of another"]. Each datum has required another to substantiate it, creating in the process this endless proliferation of "texto sobre texto." As she considers the problem, she becomes aware, moreover, that it is much more than a mere question of volume: "Siempre hay un texto soñado, indeciso y fugaz, anterior al que de verdad se recita, barrido por él" (p. 40) ["There is always a text that is but a dream, vague and ephemeral, preceding and erased by the one that is actually being quoted"]. Apparently the act of placing these static documents into the context of dynamic personal experience leads to a network of associations; the documents are transformed into texts, and each text, "being the intertext of another text, belongs to the intertextual."[9]

The protagonist's memory serves as entrance into this intertextual network. In spite of the copious documentation she has collected, her memory refuses to submit itself to even the most elementary temporal division: "Yo es que la guerra y la posguerra las recuerdo siempre confundidas. Por eso me resulta difícil escribir el libro" (p. 127) ["I am always confusing in my mind the war and the postwar period. That's the reason it is so difficult for me to write the book"]. The factual history recorded in her notes is in obvious conflict with her personal experience of this history. For example, when the stranger asks her to recount a specific event she had mentioned, her memory forges its own path: "Hago un leve gesto de asentimiento, que no se refiere para nada a ese texto del año cincuenta y tres por el que parece interesarse, sino que retrocede a sus fuentes" (p. 48) ["I nod agreement, which has nothing at all to do with the text of 1953 that he seems to be interested in, but rather slips back to its sources"]. But this constant movement toward the source is not a question of identifying influences or references—for every source identified there will always be another source. Her mind is responding to free associations triggered by the stranger's questions. Each fragment from the past is traversed by a network of intertextual associations placing her memory in constant conflict with an orderly presentation of historical facts; her attempts to write a book of memories as a factual account are opposed by the subjective essence of personal experience, by the unrelenting force of intertextuality.

Factual accounts require the use of historical narrative, or the presentation of events in their proper sequence without intervention by the enunciator or narrator; historical narrative is impersonal since it excludes every "autobiographical" linguistic form.[10] The inadequacy of such a narrative mode to convey her personal experiences is apparent when she explains to the stranger why she has not even begun to write her memoirs: "Se me enfrió, me lo enfriaron las memorias ajenas. Desde la muerte de Franco habrá notado cómo proliferan los libros de memorias, ya es una peste, en el fondo, eso es lo que me ha venido desanimando, pensar que, si a mí me aburren las memorias de los demás, por qué no les van a aburrir a los demás las mías" (p. 128) ["The project just stopped cold on me, other people's memoirs stopped me cold. Since the death of Franco you have probably noticed how books of memoirs have proliferated to the point it is now a plague. To go right to the core of things, the thought that has been discouraging me all along is that if other people's memoirs bore me, why aren't mine going to bore them"]. By attempting to limit herself to a narrative mode that is in direct conflict with the subjective essence of memories, she has stifled her creative instincts; she is attempting to reduce to impersonal narration her personal experiences. Apparently for this reason the stranger advises her: "No lo escriba en plan de libro de memorias" (p. 128) ["Don't write it in the form of a book of memoirs"]. But as soon as she promises him she will follow his advice, she remembers another promise she made: "En seguida de decirlo, pienso que eso mismo le prometí a Todorov en enero. Claro que entonces se trataba de una novela fantástica. Se me acaba de ocurrir una idea. ¿Y si mezclara las dos promesas en una?" (p. 128) ["As soon as I say it, I remember that I promised Todorov the same thing last January. Of course that was a question of a novel in the fantastic mode. I have just had an idea. Why not combine the two promises into one?"]. The protagonist's decision to abandon historical narrative as a mode for writing her book is a reflection, of course, of the very process in which she is involved as a narrator who really isn't narrating. Rather than telling a story composed of a sequential plot line—historical narrative—she is discussing how to go about composing a story. Indeed, her problem is precisely how to make the episodes she wants to include in the story conform to a sequential order, and of course how to keep her autobiographical linguistic forms out of it. Now suddenly Todorov's concept of the fantastic offers itself as an opportune vehicle for justifying the very narrative mode she can't avoid anyway.

Todorov actually imposes himself on the protagonist well before the preceding example and in a much more physical manner:

Ahí está el libro que me hizo perder pie: *Introducción a la literatura fantástica* de Todorov, vaya, a buenas horas, lo estuve buscando ante no sé cuanto rato, habla de los desdoblamientos de personalidad, de la ruptura de límites entre tiempo y espacio, de la ambigüedad y la incertidumbre; es de esos libros que te espabilan y te disparan a tomar notas, cuando lo acabé, escribí en un cuaderno: "Palabra que voy a escribir una novela fantástica", supongo que se lo prometía a Todorov. [p. 19]

[There's the book that made me trip: *Introduction to Fantastic Literature* by Todorov, how about that, it's about time, I was looking for it for I don't know how long. It deals with personality bifurcation, with a breakdown between temporal and spatial limits, with ambiguity and uncertainty; it's one of those books that excite you and make you rush to take notes, and when I finished it, I wrote in a notebook: "I swear I am going to write a novel in the fantastic mode," I suppose that I was promising it to Todorov.]

In effect, character bifurcation, a breakdown between temporal and spatial limits, and ambiguity and uncertainty are precisely the phenomena interfering with the protagonist's efforts to construct a historical narrative. Yet it takes the mysterious stranger, a person whose very appearance on the scene and whose enigmatic background reflect what Todorov defines as the fantastic, to allow her to recognize the striking similarity between such a mode and her own literary inclinations.

Not only do the protagonist's literary inclinations form an affinity with the fantastic mode, but her discursive interaction with the stranger forms a part of the fantastic. For example, when reconstructing in her own mind a romantic encounter from the past she finally says to herself: "Esto es la literatura. Me está habitando la literatura" (p. 49) ["That's a pure literary conceit. Literary conceits are overpowering me"]. Although these are clearly her inner thoughts, the stranger replies and even helps her construct the anecdote:

—Lo más logrado—dice el hombre—es la sensación de extrañeza. Usted llega con su acompañante, se apoyan juntos contra la barandilla de aquel puente a mirar el río verde con el molino al fondo, ahí ya está contenido el germen de lo fantástico, y durante toda la primera parte consigue mantenerlo. Ese hombre que va con usted no se sabe si existe o no existe, si la conoce bien o no, eso es lo verdaderamente esencial, atreverse a desafiar la incertidumbre; y el lector siente que no puede creerse ni dejarse de creer lo que vaya a pasar en adelante, ésa es la base de la literatura de misterio, se trata de un rechazo a todo lo que luego, en aquel hotel, se empeña en manifestarse ante usted como normal y evidente, ¿no? [pp. 49-50]

[—The most effective aspect—the man says—is the sensation of strangeness. You arrive with your companion, the two of you lean against the railing of that bridge to look at the green river with the mill in the background, and right there is the core of the fantastic mode, and during the whole first part you succeed in maintaining it. One does not know if that man you are with really exists or not, if he knows you well or not, and that is what is absolutely essential, to dare to defy uncertainty; and the reader feels that he cannot allow himself to believe or not believe whatever happens next, that is the foundation of mysterious literature, it is a question of rejecting everything that later, in that hotel, insists on presenting itself before you as normal and evident, don't you agree?]

The stranger's advice to incorporate unresolved mystery into her story merely reflects the unresolved mystery she is now involved in as she talks to him, or rather as he responds to her inner thoughts. In short, he is demonstrating to her that the fantastic is indeed a dimension of her reality, and not merely an escape from it.

The stranger's lesson is reinforced by the protagonist's emerging self-awareness, most apparent when she remembers the day she began writing historical books: "una tarde de sol, cuando había empezado a refugiarme en la historia, en las fechas" (p. 59) ["one sunny afternoon, when I began to take refuge in history, in dates"]. Rather than a confrontation with reality, she is beginning to realize that documented history can be a type of escapism (a type of escapism that may well point to the so-called social realist writers of the 1950s and 1960s as well as to her personal circumstances).[11] But according to the stranger, an even greater danger of documentation is the assumption that literature must conform to its rules of cause and effect, for as he notes: "La literatura es un desafío a la lógica . . . no un refugio contra la incertidumbre" (p. 55) ["Literature is a defiance of logic . . . not a refuge against uncertainty"]. He goes on to explain to her how the fantastic reflects reality: "cosas raras pasan a cada momento. El error está en que nos empeñamos en aplicarles la ley de la gravitación universal, o la ley del reloj, o cualquier otra ley de las que acatamos habitualmente sin discusión; se nos hace duro admitir que tengan ellas su propia ley" (p. 103) ["unusual things happen all the time. The error lies in insisting upon applying to them the law of universal gravitation, or the law of clocks, or any other laws that we routinely obey without challenge; it becomes difficult for us to admit that they operate by their own laws"]. Thanks to the discursive exchange she is engaged in with her addressee, the protagonist is slowly realizing that fantastic literature frees both writer and reader from a one-dimensional, cause-and-effect view of existence. And as she begins to recognize the illogical phasis of the universe, she also begins to recognize the role of language in such a universe.

In effect, language in its static written form has been the real obstacle to her creative impulses: "Siempre el mismo afán de apuntar cosas que parecen urgentes, siempre garabateando palabras sueltas en papeles sueltos, en cuadernos, y total para qué, en cuanto veo mi letra escrita, las cosas a que se refiere el texto se convierten en mariposas disecadas que antes estaban volando al sol . . . vivo rodeada de papeles sueltos donde he pretendido en vano cazar fantasmas y retener recados importantes" (pp. 121-22) ["Always the same obsession with jotting down things that seem urgent, always scribbling isolated words on separate pieces of paper, in notebooks, and when everything is said and done, for what, as soon as I see my handwriting, the things to which the text refers are converted into disected butterflies that earlier were flying around the sun . . . I am surrounded by loose pieces of paper on which I have attempted in vain to capture ghosts and preserve important messages"]. Static markers on a page attempting to stand for dynamic experience constitute the problem.

Yet language cannot stand for anything other than itself. Word and thought, image and object, sign and meaning can never become one, even though mimetic representation tends to make it appear so. But as Todorov himself notes, the fantastic mode provides a solution to the ossifying effect of mimetic representation by unmasking the illusion that language can stand for reality: "If the fantastic constantly makes use of rhetorical figures, it is because it originates in them. The supernatural is born of language, it is both its consequence and its proof: not only do the devil and vampires exist only in words, but language alone enables us to conceive what is always absent: the supernatural. The supernatural thereby becomes a symbol of language, just as the figures of rhetoric do."[12] The fantastic mode, therefore, merely underscores the essence of all literature: a fantasy world composed of language. By thus freeing language from the illusion that it is what it represents, the fantastic mode foregrounds the transformation of the static markers on the page into a plethora of interconnecting texts in dynamic discourse with one another.

Discourse, finally, is the force capable of solving the protagonist's need for a new mode of artistic expression. When, for example, she laments to the stranger that the book they have been discussing does not even exist, he reassures her by explaining: "Si ya fuera un libro no nos estaríamos divirtiendo tanto esta noche, las cosas sólo valen mientras se están haciendo, ¿no cree? . . . Además contar cómo se le ha ocurrido ya es como empezar a escribirlo, aunque nunca lo escriba, que eso ¡qué más da!" (p. 129) ["If it were already a book we wouldn't be having such a good time tonight, things are only worth while in the process of doing them, don't you agree? . . . Besides, to tell how it came to you is just like beginning to write it, and although you may never write it, so what!"]. Thus *El cuarto de atrás* separates the written artifact, which within the fiction exists only as the stack of papers on the table in the corner, from the activity of producing texts through discourse. And since discourse involves "an utterance assuming a speaker and a hearer, and in the speaker, the intention of influencing the other in some way,"[13] the text addressee plays a role as creative as that of the protagonist. Furthermore, in this case the text reader is also a text speaker. The protagonist, apparently sensing her interlocutor's essential role in the creative process when she summoned him in the first place, is acutely aware of his vital importance now as the process nears its end: "Tengo que seguir contándole cuentos, si me callo, se irá" (p. 193) ["I have to continue telling him stories, if I stop talking, he will leave me"]. The boundary separating speaker from listener does not exist in this textual situation; one is as important as the other when the mode is discourse. Yet inevitably the protagonist does send away her interlocutor when, exhausted by the discussion of how to write the book and what to include in it, she falls asleep. When she does so, the text they have been jointly creating comes to an end.

As a result of the almost exclusive focus on how and what to write, the illusion is created that the written work remains an unfulfilled potential, a product yet, or perhaps never, to come into existence. Until it does come into existence, it is as if no fictional mode exists in *El cuarto de atrás*. In fact, only when the protagonist picks up the manuscript do the three worlds of the fictional mode fall into focus: "Ya estoy otra vez en la cama con el pijama azul puesto y un codo apoyado sobre la almohada. El sitio donde tenía el libro de Todorov está ocupado ahora por un bloque de folios numerados, ciento ochenta y dos. En el primero, en mayúsculas y con rotulador negro, está escrito 'EL CUARTO DE ATRAS'. Lo levanto y empiezo a leer" (p. 210) ["Here I am again in bed in my blue pajamas and one elbow leaning against the pillow. The spot where I had Todorov's book is now filled by a stack of numbered pages, one hundred and eighty-two. On the first one, in black capital letters is written the title, 'EL CUARTO DE ATRAS.' I pick it up and begin to read"]. The product that up to this point was relegated to an obscure corner now inserts itself into the forefront. And when the protagonist reads the first paragraph of the manuscript and it turns out to be the same as the paragraph with which the novel began, the fictional mode becomes clearly defined. The woman reading is now a fictive author whose narration or product she holds in her hands. By the same token the woman who earlier was talking with the stranger is now dramatically reduced to a verbal construct firmly embedded within the pages of the manuscript, as is the stranger with whom she was talking. Standing somewhere outside this written artifact is a text-act reader, whose world is on the same level but separate from that of the fictive author holding the work in her hands. A fictional mode has been created, therefore, not through the act of writing or reading but through that of discourse. Yet beyond that mode is the conventional one that makes possible this new illusion so masterfully constructed by Carmen Martín Gaite. By dramatizing her narratee and making him an active participant in discourse, by forsaking the impersonal cause-and-effect dogmas of historical narrative, and by recognizing the fantastic not only as a viable fictional mode but as an essential dimension of reality, the protagonist discovers a solution to her need for a new artistic expression. Her process of discovery, in turn, results in a novel that has been recognized as: "una de las más imaginativas respuestas de nuestra literatura a ese hecho histórico transcendente que significó la desaparición de Franco y su régimen"[14] ["one of the most imaginative replies of our literature to that transcendent historical event represented by the disappearance of Franco and his regime"]. Indeed, one reading suggested by the novel is that the reality of the Franco years cannot be apprehended by a static presentation of dates, statistics, and events; it cannot be reduced to univocal statements. The dynamic interplay of texts in *El cuarto de atrás,* on the other hand, does allow us to apprehend that the literary text is integrally woven into the sociohistorical text of the country.[15] Above all, it points toward the plurality of meanings inherent in the very concept "text": "Siempre hay un texto soñado, indeciso y fugaz, anterior al que de verdad se recita, barrido por él" (p. 40) ["There is always a text that is merely a dream, vague and ephemeral, preceding and erased by the one that is actually being cited"].

A plurality of meanings is the effect created by nearly all the textual strategies employed in the novel. When the protagonist begins to read the manuscript she earlier created, for example, her action bestows upon the original text a whole new plurality of meanings. Even the title of the novel itself points toward this liberating plurality. "El cuarto de atrás," or backroom, was the place where the protagonist as a child enjoyed the freedom to develop her creative imagination.[16] As the mature narrator attempting to come to grips with post-Franco Spain, she now sees that the present context imposes a new plurality of connotations on this text from the past: "me lo imagino también como un desván del cerebro, una especie de recinto secreto lleno de trastos borrosos, separado de las antesalas más limpias y ordenadas de la mente por una cortina que sólo se descorre de vez en cuando; los recuerdos que pueden darnos alguna sorpresa viven agazapados en el cuarto de atrás, siempre salen de allí, y sólo cuando quieren, no sirve hostigarlos" (p. 91) ["I imagine it also as an attic of the brain, a type of secret enclosure filled with dimly outlined used furniture, separated from the cleaner and more orderly front rooms of the brain by a curtain that is only pulled back once in a while; the memories capable of surprising us a little live huddled in the backroom, they always come out from there, and only when they feel like it, it does no good to try to prod them"]. Not only *El cuarto de atrás* but the whole Spanish fictional movement that emerged in the 1970s allows us to experience the lifting of this curtain with the end of the dictatorship: the freeing of the memory and of fiction itself from the shackles of historical narrative; the recognition of the fantastic as an integral part of existence; the dynamic role of discourse in the transformation of the work into a network of interconnecting texts.

Whereas in some ways the story-focused self-referential novels are the most flagrant violators of the laws of fiction, they may also herald a new direction for the Spanish novel, a movement away from the metafictional mode. For with the new prominence of the story and the blurring of the narrating act, we are but one short step from a nonmetafictional mode. Exactly what form will emerge is still unclear to this writer, but certainly it will not be a carbon copy of anything from the past. As the novel follows its spiral movement to its next stage, it will carry with it the traces of the self-referential novel, and these traces will influence whatever mode surges to the forefront, assuring in the process another unique novelistic expression.

Afterwords

Throughout this study I have defined metafiction as the violation of fictional modes, and have used that definition as the unifying focus for all the analyses. Whereas the term violation may seem somewhat extreme in some cases, I have intended it in the same sense that speech act theorists define flouting, for example, as one means of violating the Cooperative Principle.[1] Just as flouting modifies but does not destroy the speech act, so modal violations modify but do not destroy the essence of fiction. The Cooperative Principle can be violated in multiple ways and with untold effects; fictional modes can also be violated in multiple ways with untold effects. The concept, then, does not necessarily lead to a rigid, reductive formula for defining metafiction. Indeed, rather than reduce, I have attempted to demonstrate that such a concept can open the text and in so doing perhaps contribute to the community effort of discovering new dimensions of the literary experience. The efficacy of this contribution will be measured by the degree to which it inspires modifications and corrections, the degree to which the readings it offers are answered by other readings, and the degree to which the novels studied in it point to other novels.

Before the term metafiction came into vogue, critics often referred to what we now call metafictional works as anti-novels, or even non-novels. Since in my definition of metafiction I use the violation of fictional modes and conventions as the fundamental criterion, there is a certain justification for the anti- or non-novel label. Yet both have a pejorative connotation, and people who choose these labels tend to view such works as a critic's delight but a reader's ennui. They are seen as literary but not readable. For many, metafiction is guilty of one of today's most onerous crimes: elitism. Isaac Stern has provided one of the more eloquent recent replies to those who fear elitism in art:

There is another problem today: the concern about whether the arts are an elite function in a populist time. This should be faced. There's nothing wrong with the word elite; it's not a dirty word. It's a description of what the best of society can do. It does not have to carry the connotation of social and economic position. In our day, in our society, it is a recognition of what *people* can do. The world looks to the United States for leadership—political, economic, military and more. I'm sure that certain parts of Washington would be less than proud if the instruments we provided for the defense of other countries as well as our own were not the best possible airplanes, the most powerful guns, the most effective rifles and the greatest number of bullets. Why should we not have the same pride in the kind of people we develop, the organizations that represent us and the society in which we live?[2]

Although Stern's plea is obviously directed to those in the United States government and society who provide the financial support for the arts, his defense of elitism can apply to the type of literature I have examined in this study. And, I would like to argue, since in general this type of literature is elitist, it is our obligation as teachers and critics to expose our students and colleagues to it. With such a dictum I am not implying that we should abandon that other elitist group labeled the classics, or what Roland Barthes calls "readerly texts," but merely that "writerly texts" (those in which the reader in effect has to rewrite the text, in which he or she is the creator to the same degree as is the author) also have a role in our cultural development.[3] Each type of text provides its own unique aesthetic experience, and the danger is to champion one, in the name of whatever aesthetic or moral principle, to the exclusion of the other.

Of the novels examined in this study, certainly the most readerly are those from before the twentieth century. The *Quijote*, for example, is both a readerly and a writerly text, depending on the approach one applies to it. The same could be said of the Galdós novels in which the metafictional mode is prominent. But as we move into the twentieth century, the writerly tends more and more to overwhelm the readerly text; the active role of the reader becomes an explicit dimension of the work, and the role of passive consumer is all but denied. There is reason to assume, furthermore, that such a shift in emphasis reflects the change that occurred in reader expectations. Cervantes, Quevedo, and Galdós seemed to be acutely aware of reader expectations as they carefully counterbalanced the writerly dimension of their works with a more familiar readerly focus. Unamuno, on the other hand, apparently exceeded reader expectations at the time he published *Niebla;* initially considered one of his less successful novels, now it is the preferred. Each of these novelists, along with those from other countries, helped mold reader expectations to the point where the more daring metafictional expressions of the last two decades were possible. For those who accuse these recent novels of elitism, however, they too have exceeded expectations.

Forming a dramatic contrast with those who see the metafictional mode as too elitist is the school of thought that says that the current movement reflects a state of exhaustion, that solipsism has become a feeble substitute for creative imagination. Robert Scholes even goes so far as to make a moral issue of self-reflection in fiction. He believes that novelistic self-reflection projects an exaggerated sense of alienation, and that literature has an obligation to generate systems reflecting harmony between man and the natural order.[4]

That the contemporary metafictional movement is about to, if it has not already, run its course is irrefutably clear; that it should be censored by Scholes as mere "masturbatory reveling in self-scrutiny" (p. 218) seems at best an excessively sweeping generalization. Even if not fulfilling the harmonizing role Scholes would impose on them, metafictional texts reflect the society in which we exist. Even self-reflexive texts, after all, cannot escape the context in which they are created.

An explanation of the connection between the contemporary metafictional movement and Western society leads in several directions. It is possible to speculate, for example, that self-conscious narration is a reaction against our modern computerized world in which technology threatens to replace conscious creativity. It may also be a response to bureaucratic growth in all Western societies, to a need to reassert the existence of a single controlling force. Conversely, one could argue that some metafictional novels reflect the impossibility of ever identifying such a center of authority, that they are a reaction against the illusion of absolutes in any realm of human existence. Or perhaps this novelistic movement merely mirrors the leisure society Western civilization has created for itself, a society in which everything is transformed into a game and everyone is forced to play the game. Whatever explanation one offers for the relationship between metafiction and contemporary

Western society, the particular national context in which the work is created must receive prominent consideration. In the case of the Spanish self-referential novel, therefore, we should not exclude Franco Spain from our readings.

Notwithstanding the very serious danger of simplification, one must begin by recognizing that the emergence of the Spanish self-referential novel coincided with the end of the Franco dictatorship. Among the many repressive policies of the regime, what it attempted to do to language and artistic creativity seems to offer the most obvious connection between the new novelistic movement and the context from which it grew. By attempting to reduce language to a univocal ideological tool of the state through censorship, slogans, and proclamations, the dictatorship committed sodomy on language's quintessential plurality of meanings. The death of Franco in November 1975 gave added impetus to an effort already underway to restore polysemy to language; there was a new urgency to express creative freedom. As a reply, therefore, to some thirty-six years of repression, the self-referential novel signifies at least to some degree a celebration of the creative process. Perhaps that celebration of creativity more than anything else explains the switch from the earlier expression of the metafictional mode in the Spanish novel.

Rather than the former focus on the creation of illusions, the new focus is on creation itself. To whatever degree this, in addition to other factors, explains the self-referential movement, the works composing it, when read within the context in which they were created, reflect more than mere exercises in authorial self-indulgence. In one way or another they transform a unique social reality into a unique aesthetic experience. Since that social reality is in a constant process of dynamic change, the metafictional movement of the last decade is irrefutably destined to give way, if it has not already, to a new novelistic genre. Yet the end of the metafictional movement of recent times will not mark the end of metafiction. Movements are composed of a temporally-defined body of texts; modes represent atemporal strategies of expression. The metafictional mode that can be traced back at least as far as the *Quijote* certainly can be expected to prevail long after the current obsession with its textual strategies wanes.

Notes

Introduction

1. Robert Alter, *Partial Magic: The Novel as a Self-Conscious Genre* (Berkeley: Univ. of California Press, 1975).
2. Robert Scholes, "Metafiction," *Iowa Review* 1 (1970): 100-115.
3. Robert Scholes, *Fabulation and Metafiction* (Urbana: Univ. of Illinois Press, 1979).
4. Gustavo Pérez Firmat, "Metafiction Again," *Taller Literario* 1 (Fall 1980): 30-38.
5. Linda Hutcheon, *Narcissistic Narrative: The Metafictional Paradox* (Waterloo, Ontario: Wilfrid Laurier Univ. Press, 1980).
6. Inger Christensen, *The Meaning of Metafiction: A Critical Study of Selected Novels by Sterne, Nabokov, Barth, and Beckett* (Bergen: Universitetsforlaget, 1981).
7. Steven G. Kellman, *The Self-Begetting Novel* (New York: Columbia Univ. Press, 1980); John O. Stark, *The Literature of Exhaustion* (Durham: Duke Univ. Press, 1974).
8. Scholes in *Fabulation and Metafiction* suggests that we are (or were in 1979) at a turning point away from metafiction and toward a more committed movement to some degree involving or similar to science fiction. See his epilogue, entitled "Imagination Dead Imagine: Reflections on Self-Reflexive Fiction," pp. 210-18. Inger Christensen in *The Meaning of Metafiction* credits William Gass with coining the term metafiction in a collection of essays published in 1970.
9. Gérard Genette, "Genres, 'types,' modes," *Poétique* 32 (Nov. 1977): 389-421.
10. Ulrich Wicks, "The Nature of Picaresque Narrative: A Modal Approach," *PMLA* 89 (March 1974): 241.
11. Linda Hutcheon, even in her fine study on metafiction *(Narcissistic Narrative)*, confesses confusion as to how to resolve this diachronic-synchronic problem.
12. Northrop Frye, "Historical Criticism: Theory of Modes" in *Anatomy of Criticism: Four Essays* (Princeton: Princeton Univ. Press, 1957), pp. 33-67.
13. In addition to the Genette article, "Genres, 'types,' modes," see Tzvetan Todorov, *The Fantastic: A Structural Approach to a Literary Genre*, trans. Richard Howard (Ithaca: Cornell Univ. Press, 1975); and Christine Brooke-Rose, "Historical Genres/Theoretical Genres: A Discussion of Todorov on the Fantastic," *New Literary History* 13 (Autumn 1967): 145-58.
14. Robert Scholes, "Systems and System-Builders," in *Structuralism in Literature: An Introduction* (New Haven: Yale Univ. Press, 1974), pp. 117-41.
15. Christine Brooke-Rose, "Historical Genres/Theoretical Genres," for example, does a critique first of Frye and then of Todorov's "theoretical genres," noting in the latter case that Todorov also confuses historical and ahistorical criteria.

16. For one of the more recent discussion of what I am labeling "reportorial fiction," see John Hellmann, *Fables of Fact: The New Journalism as New Fiction* (Urbana: Univ. of Illinois Press, 1981). Although Hellmann sees both the "New Journalism Novel" and what he calls "fabulist fiction" as self-reflexive, he draws a basic distinction between the two similar to the one I am arguing: "The fiction writer provides such apparatus as clear fakery in order to draw attention to the traditional status of fiction as a masquerade of reality. The effect is to obviously 'frame' the work, and thus to set it off from reality. The new journalist, on the other hand, frames his work in order to convince the reader that the *opposite* is the case—that it is a 'true account' based on actual observation and years of research" (p. 14). For another theory on the transformation of referents, see John S. Brushwood, "Sobre el referente y la transformación narrativa," *Semiosis* 6 (Jan.-June 1981): 39-55.

17. John W. Kronik, "Galdós and the Grotesque," *Anales Galdosianos*, Supplement (1976): 39-54.

18. "If the fantastic constantly makes use of rhetorical figures it is because it originates in them. The supernatural is born of language, it is both its consequence and its proof: not only do the devil and vampires exist only in words, but language alone enables us to conceive what is always absent: the supernatural" (*The Fantastic*, p. 82). In his book Todorov distinguishes between "historical genres" and what he calls "theoretical genres"—the latter a mixture of generic and modal criteria. In a later article entitled "The Origin of Genres," *New Literary History* 13 (Autumn 1967): 159-70, Todorov backs away from his earlier terminology and limits his use of the term "genre" to "those classes of texts that have been perceived as such in the course of history" (p. 162). He then proposes an analysis of levels of discourse as a means of defining the properties of any given historical class of texts. In this later article Todorov seems to be echoing Genette's thesis on genre versus mode.

19. Seymour Chatman, in *Story and Discourse: Narrative Structure in Fiction and Film* (Ithaca: Cornell Univ. Press, 1978), proposes a differentiation of readers similar to what I am proposing. According to the Chatman explanation, the narratee is the addressee of the narrator, the implied reader that of the implied author, and the real reader that of the real author. As I noted earlier, the term "implied reader" can create problems since the narratee often is also implied, and in metafiction the implied reader is often given an explicit identity. Susan Sniader Lanser, *The Narrative Act: Point of View in Prose Fiction* (Princeton: Princeton Univ. Press, 1981), follows the Chatman paradigm except that she uses the word "audience" in place of "implied reader."

20. Emile Benveniste, *Problems in General Linguistics*, trans. Mary Elizabeth Meek (Coral Gables: Univ. of Miami Press, 1971), pp. 205-15 et passim.

21. In "Genres, 'types,' modes," Genette explains mode as the "situation d'énonciation" (p. 394 et passim), a term he defines in more detail as the "act of narrating" in his *Narrative Discourse: An Essay in Method*, trans. Jane E. Lewin (Ithaca: Cornell Univ. Press, 1980); see particularly his chapter "Voice," pp. 212-62.

22. Seymour Chatman, in *Story and Discourse*, defines the story as the "what of narrative" while discourse is the "way of narrative" (p. 9).

23. Genette has a term for each of these levels, but to avoid undue complications, I have chosen merely to number them. His term "metadiegetic," for example, is totally different from the way I have been using the prefix "meta" in this study.

24. For an application of the concept of narrative levels to a text see Shlomith Rimmon-Kenan, "Ambiguity and Narrative Levels: Christine Brooke-Rose's *Thru*," *Poetics Today* 3 (1982): 21-32.

25. Such a triad structure of the fictional mode basically corresponds to that proposed by Félix Martínez Bonati in a book first published in Chile in 1960 and later reprinted in Spain: *La estructura de la obra literaria: Una investigación de filosofía del lenguaje y estética* (Barcelona: Seix Barral, 1972). Recently an English version appeared as *Fictive Discourse and the Structures of Literature: A Phenomenological Approach*, trans. Philip W. Silver (Ithaca: Cornell Univ. Press, 1981).

26. Tzvetan Todorov, in "An Introduction to Verisimilitude," *The Poetics of Prose*, trans. Richard Howard (Ithaca: Cornell Univ. Press, 1977), pp. 80-88, notes a similar conflict when a writer must violate the verisimilitude of the world he is evoking in order to obey the verisimilitude of the genre in which he is writing.

Chapter One: Violations and Pseudo-Violations

1. Luis Goytisolo, in a letter to the author, 2 August 1981, states: "El *Quijote*, en efecto, y por motivos que convendría analizar, se ha convertido en 'el modelo'—no tendría sentido hablar aquí de influencias—de novela, no sólo para mí sino también para mis más destacados colegas, los Juanes, Benet, Marsé, Goytisolo."

2. The works and respective criteria for considering the *Quijote* the first modern novel are: Américo Castro, *El pensamiento de Cervantes* (Barcelona: Noguer, 1972), who cites the expression of Renaissance ideas; Dorothy Van Ghent, *The English Novel: Form and Function* (New York: Harper & Row, 1967), who quotes Lionel Trilling's thesis that all prose fiction is a variation of the theme of *Don Quijote*; José Ortega y Gasset, *Meditaciones del Quijote* (Madrid: Espasa-Calpe, 1964), who cites its ability to achieve a plurality of planes or aesthetic profundity; and Wolfgang Kayser, "Origen y crisis de la novela moderna," trans. Aurelio Fuentes Rojo, *Cultura Universitaria* 47 (1955): 5-47, who refers to the employment of a "personal narrator."

3. Alter, *Partial Magic*.

4. Miguel de Cervantes Saavedra, *El Ingenioso Hidalgo don Quijote de la Mancha* (Madrid: Espasa-Calpe, 1958), Primera Parte, Capítulo Primero, p. 47. For further citations from this edition I will note in arabic numerals Part 1 or 2, the chapter, and the page.

5. Walter J. Ong, S.J., "The Writer's Audience Is Always a Fiction," *PMLA* 90 (Jan. 1975): 9-21.

6. The thesis of Mia I. Gerhardt, *Don Quijote: La vie et les livres* (Amsterdam: N.V. Noord-Hollandsche, 1955). Gerhardt's rather obscure study has been the most influential on my own approach to the novel.

7. One might argue that an even more dramatic metafictional example occurs in Book Two when the protagonist confronts a character from Avellaneda's pla-

giarized version. Although certainly representing a violation of the world of the story, the effect of that episode strikes me as more concerned with the dispute over the plagiarized version than with the craft of fiction.

8. Francisco de Quevedo, *Historia de la vida del Buscón* (Madrid: Espasa-Calpe, 1967), p. 128.

9. The term "experiencing self" is borrowed from Franz Stanzel, *Narrative Situations in the Novel: Tom Jones, Moby-Dick, The Ambassadors, Ulysses*, trans. James P. Pusack (Bloomington: Indiana Univ. Press, 1971). Stanzel explains that the first-person narrative presents the protagonist/narrator in two dimensions. His "narrating self" is the narrator in the present in the act of telling the story. This narrating self normally has greater insight and maturity than he had at the time he experienced what he is narrating.

10. Two prominent critics, nevertheless, insist that there is a violation of narrative level. Francisco Rico, *La novela picaresca y el punto de vista* (Barcelona: Seix Barral, 1969), sees this episode as an artistic oversight in which the narrator does trespass the boundaries of his narrative. Gonzalo Díaz Migoyo, *Estructura de la novela: Anatomía de "El Buscón"* (Madrid: Editorial Fundamentos, 1978), on the other hand, believes Quevedo consciously has his narrator violate his limits in order to dramatize this key turning point. Whereas I agree that it is a conscious strategy designed to dramatize the moment, I believe that if one analyzes the point of focalization it is obviously a pseudo rather than an actual violation.

11. "The Self-Conscious Novel in Eclipse," in *Partial Magic*, pp. 84-137.

12. John W. Kronik, "*El amigo Manso* and the Game of Fictive Authority," *Anales Galdosianos* 12 (1977): 71-94.

13. John W. Kronik, "*Misericordia* as Metafiction," in *Homenaje a Antonio Sánchez Barbudo: Ensayos de literatura española moderna* (Madison: Univ. of Wisconsin Press, 1981), pp. 37- 50.

14. John W. Kronik, "Galdosian Reflections: Feijoo and the Fabrication of Fortunata," *Modern Language Notes* 97 (1982): 1-40.

15. Benito Pérez Galdós, "La de Bringas," in *Obras completas*, 6 (Madrid: Bolaños y Aguilar, 1960): 507.

16. I am indebted to Vernon A. Chamberlin for calling my attention to this story. I cite from the *Obras completas*, 6 (Madrid: Bolaños y Aguilar, 1945): 503-15.

17. A narrator interrupting to comment on the nature of what he has narrated would be an example of Gustavo Pérez Firmat's text-scholium formula as he defines it in "Metafiction Again." See my Introduction to this book for a more detailed explanation of Pérez Firmat's thesis.

18. The primary source of the theory on reader expectations is Hans Robert Jauss, "Literary History as a Challenge to Literary Theory," *New Literary History* 11 (Autumn 1970): 8-37.

Chapter Two: Fiction on a Palimpsest

1. See Lucien Dällenbach, "Intertexte et autotexte," *Poétique* 27 (1976): 282-96, for a more detailed explanation of how "mise en abysme" functions as novelistic self-commentary.

2. Leon Livingstone, *Tema y forma en las novelas de Azorín* (Madrid: Gredos, 1970), defines interior duplication in much broader terms, and discusses several works from this novelistic generation that by his definition engage in self-commentary. See particularly "El desdoblamiento interior y el problema de la forma en la novela," pp. 32- 69.

3. Prominent among such essays are: Carlos Blanco Aguinaga, "Unamuno's *Niebla:* Existence and the Game of Fiction," *MLN* 79 (1964): 188-205; José Emilio González, "Reflexiones sobre *Niebla,* de Unamuno," *Asomante* 17 (1961): 60-69; Frances W. Weber, "Unamuno's *Niebla:* From Novel to Dream," *PMLA* 88 (March 1973): 209-18; Leon Livingstone, "The Novel as Self-Creation," in *Unamuno, Creator and Creation,* ed. José Rubia Barcia and M.A. Zeitlin (Berkeley: Univ. of California Press, 1967), pp. 92-115; in the same volume, Alexander A. Parker, "On the Interpretation of *Niebla,*" pp. 116-38; and most recently, Fernando de Toro, "Personaje autónomo, lector y autor en Miguel de Unamuno," *Hispania* 64 (Sept. 1981): 360-65. For an annotated bibliography on the novel see David William Foster, *Unamuno and the Novel as Expressionistic Conceit* (Hato Rey, Puerto Rico: Inter American Univ. Press, 1973), pp. 44-52.

4. Apparently *Niebla* represents what Linda Hutcheon, in *Narcissistic Narrative,* has in mind for her metafictional linguistic mode: "the text would actually show its building blocks—the very language whose referents serve to construct that imaginative world" (pp. 28-29).

5. Miguel de Unamuno, *Niebla* (Madrid: Espasa-Calpe, 1963), p. 9.

6. Unamuno employs a similar textual strategy in *San Manuel Bueno, mártir.* As the narrator Angela describes the voice of Don Manuel when he repeats Christ's words of doubt, she notes: "Y era como si oyesen a Nuestro Señor Jesucristo mismo, como si la voz brotara de aquel viejo crucifijo a cuyos pies tantas generaciones de madres habían depositado sus congojas. Como que una vez, al oírlo su madre, la de Don Manuel . . . ." ["And it was as if they were listening to Jesus Christ himself, just as if the voice were sprouting forth from that old crucifix at whose base so many generations of mothers had deposited their griefs. So that one time, when his mother, Don Manuel's, heard it . . . ."] Miguel de Unamuno, *San Manuel Bueno, mártir* (New York: Las Americas, 1960), p. 18.

7. This is very similar to what John W. Kronik notes in reference to the prologue to Galdós's *El amigo Manso:* "The frame does not outline decoratively the image it contains or simply circumscribe that image spatially; instead, it infuses the construct with meaning and delimits that meaning. It is a sign superimposed on another sign, which latter can no longer be perceived independently of its informing structure" (pp. 74-75). "*El amigo Manso* and the Game of Fictive Autonomy," *Anales Galdosianos* 12 (1977): 71-94.

8. For the reasons just outlined I take issue with Robert Alter, *Partial Magic,* when, after first conceding that *Niebla* raises questions that might be regarded as prolegomena for the self-conscious novel in the twentieth century, Alter concludes by saying: "The problem with Unamuno's novel—it is a recurrent trap for modern self- conscious novelists—is that nothing in its fictional realization is quite so interesting as the theorizing that goes on within it" (p. 157).

Notes to Pages 45-47

Chapter Three: Codes versus Modes

1. For a more detailed discussion of Spanish vanguardism, see: Miguel Angel Hernández, *Prosa vanguardista en la generación del 27 (Gecé y La Gaceta Literaria)* (Madrid: Prensa Española, 1975); Ramón Buckley and John Crispin, *Los vanguardistas españoles (1925-1935)* (Madrid: Alianza, 1973); and especially Gustavo Pérez Firmat, *Idle Fictions: The Hispanic Vanguard Novel, 1926-1934* (Durham: Duke Univ. Press, 1983). The accuracy of the rubric "art for art's sake" for vanguardism has been challenged by at least one critic: Víctor Fuentes, "La narrativa española de vanguardia (1923-1931): Un ensayo de interpretación," *Romanic Review* 63 (Oct. 1972): 211-18.

2. A sampling of critics' reactions to Jarnés's novels: Eugenio de Nora, *La novela española contemporánea*, vol. 2 (Madrid: Gredos, 1962): "Lo característico de Jarnés y sus coetáneos es, precisamente, la desmembración sistemática y—en cierta medida—la reconstrucción artificial y laberíntica del relato. El artista suplanta, o cuando menos somete abiertamente al creador; la habilidad pasa a ser mucho más necesaria e importante que la inventiva" (p. 155). Emilia de Zuleta, *Arte y vida en la obra de Benjamín Jarnés* (Madrid: Gredos, 1977): "Los personajes o el narrador, dentro de la novela o en unidades narrativas menores introducidas ex profeso, toman a su cargo la tarea de advertir al público y a los críticos sobre las interpretaciones que del género se han hecho en cada caso particular, sobre los fines de la novela, sobre la selección de las técnicas utilizadas y sobre muchos aspectos más" (p. 115). Víctor Fuentes, "La dimensión estético-erótica y la novelística de Jarnés," *Cuadernos Hispanoamericanos* 235 (July 1969): 25-37: "La narrativa de Jarnés halla principal soporte en la propia intimidad del autor—de aquí su marcado carácter lírico y ensayístico—, quien se proyecta en su obra, en el papel del poeta, como liberador y creador que aspira a establecer un orden más alto en el mundo, fundado en la armonía y la fratificación y no en la supresión" (p. 28). Joaquín de Entrambasaguas, *Las mejores novelas contemporáneas*, vol. 7 (Barcelona: Planeta, 1961): "Y el hombre, las actitudes del hombre ante el mundo que le rodea, sus reacciones individuales, serán los temas de las novelas de Benjamín Jarnés, en que él mismo figurará directamente—Julio—o dentro de sus personajes . . . porque a través de ellos expone teorías sistemáticas" (p. 1334). In the most recent monographic study of Jarnés's work, María Pilar Martínez Latre, *La novela intelectual de Benjamín Jarnés* (Zaragoza: Institución Fernando el Católico, 1979), comments: "La búsqueda de una expresión original le obliga a utilizar un lenguaje esotérico, propenso a las brillantes y sugestivas metáforas, que lo alejan de la trivialidad, pero dificultan la comprensión del mensaje (descoyuntan la trama novelesca y la atomizan)" (p. 27).

3. Paul Ilie, "Benjamín Jarnés: Aspects of the Dehumanized Novel," *PMLA* 76 (1961): 247-53, has made by far the most insightful study of "dehumanization" in Jarnés's novels.

4. Gustavo Pérez Firmat, "*Locura y muerte de nadie:* Two Novels by Jarnés," *Romanic Review* 72 (1981): 66-78.

5. I am following Oswald Ducrot and Tzvetan Todorov in defining literary codes as the system of formal constraints distinguishing the different literary movements, genres, and styles: *Dictionnaire encyclopédique des sciences du langage* (Paris: Editions du Seuil, 1972), p. 137.

6. Benjamín Jarnés, "Locura y muerte de nadie" in *Las mejores novelas contemporáneas*, vol. 7 (Barcelona: Planeta, 1961) ed. Joaquín de Entrambasaguas, p. 1426.

7. For an example of a narrator of a Jarnés novel directly addressing a character, see *Teoría del zumbel* (Madrid: Espasa-Calpe, 1930), pp. 47-53.

8. Such an explanation basically corresponds to how Mikhail Bakhtin defines parody in his *Problems of Dostoevsky's Poetics*, trans. R.W. Rotsel (Ann Arbor: Ardis, 1973). See particularly the chapter entitled "The Word in Dostoevsky," pp. 150-227.

9. For a much more detailed explanation of focalization, see Mieke Bal, "Narration et focalisation: Pour une théorie des instances du récit," *Poétique* 29 (1977): 107-27.

10. "Apuntes para un modelo de la intertextualidad en literatura," *Romanic Review* 69 (1978): 1-14. Bakhtin says the borrowed words become "double voiced" when introduced into someone else's speech (*Problems of Dostoevsky's Poetics*, p. 161).

11. There is, however, one notable exception in *Locura y muerte de nadie* where the modes of fiction are violated. At the end of chapter thirteen, after Juan's failure to catch Matilde and Arturo in a compromising position, which would enable him to avenge his honor in truly noble tradition, the narrator notes: "En este breve relato, en este fragmento de la vida de Juan Sánchez, no se tuvo la fortuna de hallar a todos los personajes en su punto de más alta tensión. Para alguno se adelantó, para otro se retrasó la novela" (p. 1504). ["In this brief story, in this fragment from the life of Juan Sánchez, one was not fortunate enough to catch all of the characters at their highest point of dramatic tension. For some the novel got ahead of itself, for others it fell behind."] He is saying, in effect, that the novel has betrayed him, that as author he has no control over it. This is an example, of course, of a violation of the laws of fiction, although the intent seems more playful and less probing than, say, what we saw in Unamuno. At any rate such an example is an exception rather than a rule in this particular novel.

12. J.S. Bernstein, *Benjamín Jarnés* (New York: Twayne, 1972), p. 100.

13. Benjamín Jarnés, *La novia del viento* (Mexico City: Nueva Cultura, 1940), p. 58.

14. Emilia de Zuleta, *Arte y vida*, p. 236, reports that a copy of this painting is in fact listed in the Prado catalogue and is also reproduced in the *Encyclopedia Espasa*.

15. Gustavo Pérez Firmat, "Pedro Salinas' 'Mundo cerrado' and Hispanic Vanguard Fiction," *La Chispa '81: Selected Proceedings* (New Orleans: Tulane Univ., 1982), pp. 261-67, perspicuously analyzes how the Salinas short story "Mundo cerrado" reflects one of Ortega y Gasset's metaphors on the "new art." According to Ortega in his famous essay *La deshumanización del arte* (Madrid: Revista de Occidente, 1925), the problem of separating the artistic work from its content, i.e., story, is similar to the problem of viewing a scene through a window pane. One must either focus on the pane and thereby blot out the scene, or focus on the scene thereby ignoring the existence of the window pane. Ortega argues that the "new art" blots out the story so as to direct attention to the artistic work. The foregrounding of literary codes seems to characterize a basic vanguardist strategy for switching the focus from the content to the work of art.

16. Alter, *Partial Magic*, p. xii-xiii.

17. Since this essay was written, a collection of previously published articles on Jarnés has appeared, *La novela lírica, II: Pérez de Ayala, Jarnés*, ed. Darío Villanueva

(Madrid: Taurus, 1983). Several of the articles in Villanueva's volume are cited in this chapter.

Chapter Four: Rebellion against Models

1. J.M. Martínez Cachero, *La novela española entre 1939 y 1969* (Madrid: Editorial Castalia, 1973), has best documented the continuing novelistic activity of the war years.

2. Other terms applied to this novelistic movement include social realism, objective realism, behaviorism, *Tremendismo*, and variations mixing or modifying with other adjectives the terms listed. For the best panoramic studies of the postwar Spanish novel see: Gonzalo Sobejano, *Novela española de nuestro tiempo (En busca del pueblo perdido)* (Madrid: Editorial Prensa Española, 1970); and Ignacio Soldevila Durante, *La novela desde 1936* (Madrid: Alhambra, 1980).

3. Alter, *Partial Magic*, obviously unaware of Galdós, sees a similar hiatus in the nineteenth-century realist novel. Alter attributes such a hiatus to the realist novel's function as a source of sociopolitical information (see "The Self-Conscious Novel in Eclipse" pp. 84-137).

4. Gustavo Pérez Firmat, indeed, argues that Ignacio Aldecoa's neorealistic *El fulgor y la sangre* (1954) is an example of "narrative metafiction," or a type of novel whose metafictionality is conveyed allegorically. Such an open definition of metafiction does not correspond to my use of the term in this study. See Pérez Firmat's "Metafiction Again."

5. The best studies comparing neorealism and the New Novel are: Janet W. Díaz, "Origins, Aesthetics and the 'Nueva Novela Española,' " *Hispania* 59 (March 1976): 109-17; and Félix Grande, "Narrativa, realidad y España actuales: Historia de un amor difícil," *Cuadernos Hispanoamericanos* 101 (May 1975): 545-51.

6. I present this thesis with various examples in my article "El nuevo lenguaje de la nueva novela," *Insula* 396-97 (Nov.-Dec. 1979): 6-7.

7. Gonzalo Torrente Ballester, *Don Juan* (Barcelona: Destino, 1963), p. 20.

8. See, for example: Michael D. Thomas, "Cunqueiro's *Un hombre que se parecía a Orestes*: A Humorous Revitalization of an Ancient Myth," *Hispania* 61 (March 1978): 35-45; Pacho Marinero, "Don Alvaro de Bretaña: Perífrasis y paráfrasis del tiempo," *Insula* 308-9 (July-Aug. 1972): 23; César Antonio Molina, "Alvaro Cunqueiro: La fabulación sin fin," *Insula* 413 (April 1981): 1, 10-11; and Jacqueline Eyring Bixler, "Self-Conscious Narrative and Metatheatre in *Un hombre que se parecía a Orestes*," *Hispania* 67 (May 1984): 214-20.

9. I discuss how the sketch of Orestes complements the general treatment of the myth in "Mito-realidad: La dinámica de *Un hombre que se parecía a Orestes*"in *La novela española de posguerra: Creación artística y experiencia personal* (Madrid: CUPSA, 1978), 246-77.

10. Alvaro Cunqueiro, *Un hombre que se parecía a Orestes* (Barcelona: Destino, 1969), p. 24.

11. Bixler, "Self-Conscious Narrative," in defending the Doña Inés section, argues that indeed it contributes to the novel's structural unity. One might argue

Notes to Pages 70-82 137

that the chorus in the *Oresteia* was itself a metafictional device, perhaps even an inspiration for Cunqueiro's experiments with the mode.

Chapter Five: Process as Product

1. I first proposed this term in my article "From Neorealism and the New Novel to the Self-Referential Novel: Juan Goytisolo's *Juan sin Tierra*," *Anales de la Narrativa Española Contemporánea* 5 (1980): 73-82.

2. (Barcelona: Seix Barral, 1973). For the most insightful essay written to date on the novel, see: David K. Herzberger, "Luis Goytisolo's *Recuento:* Towards a Reconciliation of the Word/World Dialectic," *Anales de la Novela de Posguerra* 3 (1978): 39-55.

3. (Barcelona: Seix Barral, 1976). I am aware of only two articles to date on this novel: Alexandra Riccio, "De las ruinas al taller en la obra de Luis Goytisolo," *Anales de la Novela de Posguerra* 2 (1977): 31-42; and José Ortega, "Aspectos narrativos en *Los verdes de mayo hasta el mar*, de Luis Goytisolo," *Cuadernos Hispanoamericanos* 370 (April 1981): 105-14.

4. There are several important essays on this novel, including a whole collection entitled *Juan sin Tierra* (Madrid: Espiral/Revista, 1977), edited by Julián Ríos. Also of note are: Susan F. Levine, " 'Cuerpo' y 'no-cuerpo'—Una conjunción entre Juan Goytisolo y Octavio Paz," *Journal of Spanish Studies: Twentieth Century* 5 (Fall 1977): 123-35; and Michael Ugarte, *Trilogy of Treason: An Intertextual Study of Juan Goytisolo* (Columbia: Univ. of Missouri Press, 1981). My own previous work on this novel can be found in, "Latrines, Whirlpools, and Voids: The Metafictional Mode of *Juan sin Tierra*," *Hispanic Review* 48 (Spring 1980): 151-69; and reprinted in translation in *Voces* 1 (1982): 67-79, as "Letrinas, torbellinos y vacíos: el modo metaficcional de *Juan sin Tierra*"; and the article on the self-referential novel cited in note 1 of this chapter.

5. In this essay I have adopted the term text author to distinguish between the fictive author whose explicit appearance always constitutes a violation, and the character/author within the story such as Raúl in *Los verdes de mayo hasta el mar*. Since the text author of *Juan sin Tierra* both assumes responsibility for writing the work and projects himself into the story as a character, I want to distinguish between the two previously used terms.

6. Juan Goytisolo, *Juan sin Tierra* (Barcelona: Seix Barral, 1975), pp. 312-13.

7. From Roland Barthes, "Textual Analysis of a Tale by Edgar Poe," *Poe Studies* 10 (June 1977): 1-12, I am borrowing the term and concept "narrative code."

8. Susan F. Levine, " 'Cuerpo' y 'no-cuerpo,' " discusses several interesting implications of the digestive process and how Goytisolo incorporates some of Octavio Paz's concepts on the subject into the novel.

9. Throughout the novel the text author draws semiotic connections between artistic creativity and Western bourgeois values: "antes de que la vieja predisposición de la estirpe a suprimir la libertad viva de hoy en nombre de la imaginaria libertad de mañana sometiese la invención creadora a los imperativos de la producción" (p. 14) ["before the old predisposition of the race to suppress the living liberty

of today in the name of the imaginary liberty of tomorrow subjects creative invention to the imperatives of production"].

10. I am borrowing the dream analogy from Mieke Bal's definition of third-degree focalization; see his "Narration et focalisation."

11. According to Goytisolo, the translation of the Arabic script is: "estoy definitivamente al otro lado, con los parias de siempre, afilando el cuchillo" ["I am definitively on the other side, with the eternal pariahs, sharpening my knife"]. See "Juan Goytisolo-Julián Ríos: Desde *Juan sin Tierra*," p. 10 in the collection of essays on the novel (see note 4 of this chapter).

12. Readers represent the interesting contradiction of tremendous freedom of interpretation tempered always by the constraints imposed by the text. As Inge Crosman explains, in "Poétique de la lecture romanesque," *L'Esprit Créateur* 21 (Summer 1981): 70-80: "La lecture conçue ainsi est un rôle à jouer par un lecteur plus ou moins libre, plus ou moins contraint selon le programme prévu par le texte" (p. 71).

13. As I hope my argument has shown, it is misleading to equate the text author with the real author Juan Goytisolo. Some people may be led to believe, for example, that when the text author notes near the end of the novel that, "si en lo futuro escribes, será en otra lengua" (p. 319) ["if you write in the future, it will be in another language"], Goytisolo contradicts himself by then publishing *Makbara* in Spanish. The only contradiction lies in equating the words of a fictitious creation with those of a real person.

Chapter Six: Reading-into-Being

1. Gonzalo Torrente Ballester, *Fragmentos de Apocalipsis* (Barcelona: Destino, 1977), p. 82.

2. Javier Tomeo, *El castillo de la carta cifrada* (Barcelona: Anagrama, 1979), p. 5.

3. Luis Goytisolo, *La cólera de Aquiles* (Barcelona: Seix Barral, 1979), p. 296.

4. Martínez Bonati, *Fictive Discourse and the Structures of Literature*. See especially "Statification of the Literary Work According to the Various Logical Kinds of Discourse," pp. 27-43.

5. I am not aware of any critical article to date on this novel other than my own much abridged and somewhat differently focused essay "*La cólera de Aquiles:* Un texto producto del lector," *Revista Iberoamericana* 47 (July-Dec. 1981): 241-45; and Gonzalo Sobejano's "El 'Ecce Homo' de Matilde Moret" in *El cosmos de "Antagonía": Incursiones en la obra de Luis Goytisolo*, prologue by Salvador Clotas (Barcelona: Editorial Anagrama, 1983), pp. 89-106.

Chapter Seven: Product Preceding Process

1. "Juan Goytisolo-Julián Ríos: Desde *Juan sin Tierra*," in *Juan sin Tierra* (Madrid: Espiral/Revista, 1977), p. 11.

2. Juan Goytisolo, *Makbara* (Barcelona: Seix Barral, 1980), p. 221.

3. Not surprisingly, since Juan Goytisolo is the author, *Makbara* has already

generated a considerable amount of criticism. See, in the special issue of *Revista Iberoamericana* 116-17 (July-Dec. 1981), the following articles: Gonzalo Sobejano, "Valores figurativos y compositivos de la soledad en la novela de Juan Goytisolo," pp. 81-88; Maryellen Bieder, "De *Señas de identidad* a *Makbara*: Estrategia narrativa en las novelas de Juan Goytisolo," pp. 89-96; Linda Gould Levine, "*Makbara*: Entre la espada y la pared—¿política marxista o política sexual?" pp. 97-106. In addition, see the special issue of *Voces* 1 (1981), particularly Malika Jdidi Embarec, "Lectura marroquí de *Makbara*," pp. 83-86.

4. Luis Goytisolo, *Teoría del conocimiento* (Barcelona: Seix Barral, 1981), p. 29.

5. For more views on *Antagonía* see: *El cosmos de "Antagonía"*.

6. Roland Barthes, "From Work to Text," in *Textual Strategies: Perspectives in Post-Structuralist Criticism*, ed. Josué V. Harari (Ithaca: Cornell Univ. Press, 1979), pp. 73-81.

7. Carmen Martín Gaite, *El cuarto de atrás* (Barcelona: Destino, 1978), p. 25.

8. It is difficult to ignore an echo here from Galdós's *Misericordia* in which the protagonist invents a priest to explain the food she manages to provide for her destitute mistress, the priest later appearing as a character in the novel.

9. Barthes, "From Work to Text," p. 77.

10. For a more detailed definition of historical narrative see Emile Benveniste, "The Correlations of Tense in the French Verb," in *Problems in General Linguistics*, pp. 205-15.

11. There is an obvious correlation here between the protagonist's life and that of the real author. Martín Gaite interrupted her own novelistic career to do studies on Macanaz and on love in eighteenth-century Spain. The novelist, however, has made it clear that she incorporates autobiographical data into a fictional context. In other words, the novel is not a history of her life but a fictional creation drawing from certain real episodes. See Marie-Lise Gazarian Gautier, "Conversación con Carmen Martín Gaite en Nueva York," *Insula* 411 (Feb. 1981): 1, 10-11.

12. Todorov, *The Fantastic*, p. 82.

13. Benveniste, "Correlations of Tense," pp. 205-15.

14. Darío Villanueva, "La novela española en 1978," *Anales de la Narrativa Española Contemporánea* 4 (1979): 93.

15. The concept of intertextuality, as I am applying it, corresponds to my reading of Julia Kristeva's explanation, for example as in "The Bound Text," in *Desire in Language: A Semiotic Approach to Literature and Art*, trans. Thomas Gora et al. (New York: Columbia Univ. Press, 1980), pp. 36-63. See also Jonathan Culler's "Presupposition and Intertextuality," in *The Pursuit of Signs: Semiotics, Literature, Deconstruction* (Ithaca: Cornell Univ. Press, 1981), pp. 100-118.

16. For other readings of the novel see: Blas Matamoro, "Carmen Martín Gaite: El viaje al cuarto de atrás," *Cuadernos Hispanoamericanos* 351 (Sept. 1979): 581-605; and Julián Palley, "El interlocutor soñado de *El cuarto de atrás*, de Carmen Martín Gaite," *Insula* 404-5 (July-Aug. 1980): 22. From the collection *From Fiction to Metafiction: Essays in Honor of Carmen Martín-Gaite*, ed. Mirella Servodidio and Marcia L. Welles (Lincoln: Society of Spanish and Spanish-American Studies, 1983), see the following: Julián Palley, "Dreams in Two Novels of Carmen Martín Gaite," pp. 107-16; Mirella d'Ambrosio Servodidio, "Oneiric Intertextualities," pp. 117-27; Manuel Durán, "*El cuarto de atrás*: Imaginación, fantasía, misterio;

Todorov y algo más," pp. 129-37; Robert C. Spires, "Intertextuality in *El cuarto de atrás*," pp. 139-48; Kathleen M. Glenn, "*El cuarto de atrás:* Literature as *Juego* and the Self-Reflexive Text," p. 159; Linda Gould Levine, "Carmen Martín Gaite's *El cuarto de atrás:* A Portrait of the Artist as Woman," pp. 161-72; Ruth El Saffar, "Liberation and the Labyrinth: A Study of the Works of Carmen Martín Gaite," pp. 185-96; Marcia L. Welles, "Carmen Martín Gaite: Fiction as Desire," pp. 197-207; and Gonzalo Sobejano, "Enlaces y desenlaces en las novelas de Carmen Martín Gaite," pp. 209-23.

Afterwords

1. The best explanation of speech act theory as it applies to literature can be found in Mary Louis Pratt, *Toward a Speech Act Theory of Literary Discourse* (Bloomington: Indiana Univ. Press, 1977).

2. Isaac Stern, quoted in *Wall Street Journal*, 16 Oct. 1981, p. 25.

3. Roland Barthes, *S/Z: An Essay*, trans. Richard Howard (New York: Hill and Wang, 1974), pp. 3-4 et passim.

4. *Fabulation and Metafiction*, pp. 215-18.

Bibliography

Theory

Alter, Robert. *Partial Magic: The Novel as a Self-Conscious Genre.* Berkeley: University of California Press, 1975.

Bakhtin, Mikhail. *Problems of Dostoevsky's Poetics.* Translated by R.W. Rotsel. Ann Arbor: Ardis, 1973.

Bal, Mieke. "Narration et focalisation: Pour une théorie des instances du récit." *Poétique* 29 (1977): 107-27.

Barthes, Roland. "From Work to Text." In *Textual Strategies: Perspectives in Post-Structuralist Criticism,* edited by Josué V. Harari, pp. 73-81. Ithaca: Cornell University Press, 1979.

———. *S/Z: An Essay.* Translated by Richard Howard. New York: Hill and Wang, 1974.

———. "Textual Analysis of a Tale by Edgar Poe." *Poe Studies* 10 (June 1977): 1-12.

———. *Writing Degree Zero.* Translated by Annette Lavers and Colin Smith. New York: Hill and Wang, 1968.

Benveniste, Emile. *Problems in General Linguistics.* Translated by Mary Elizabeth Meck. Coral Gables: University of Miami Press, 1971.

Booth, Wayne. *The Rhetoric of Fiction.* Chicago: University of Chicago Press, 1961.

Brooke-Rose, Christine. "Historical Genres/Theoretical Genres: A Discussion of Todorov on the Fantastic." *New Literary History* 13 (Autumn 1967): 145-58.

Brushwood, John S. "Sobre el referente y la transformación narrativa." *Semiosis* 6 (1981): 39-55.

Chatman, Seymour. *Story and Discourse: Narrative Structure in Fiction and Film.* Ithaca: Cornell University Press, 1978.

Christensen, Inger. *The Meaning of Metafiction: A Critical Study of Selected Novels by Sterne, Nabokov, Barth, and Beckett.* Bergen: Universitetsforlaget, 1981.

Crosman, Inge. "Poétique de la lecture romanesque." *L'Esprit Créateur* 21 (Summer 1981): 70-80.

Culler, Jonathan. *The Pursuit of Signs: Semiotics, Literature, Deconstruction.* Ithaca: Cornell University Press, 1981.

───. *Structuralist Poetics: Structuralism, Linguistics, and the Study of Literature.* Ithaca: Cornell University Press, 1975.

Dallenbach, Lucien. "Intertexte et autotexte." *Poétique* 27 (1976): 282-96.

De Man, Paul. *Allegories of Reading: Figural Language in Rousseau, Nietzsche, Rilke, Proust.* New Haven: Yale University Press, 1979.

Derrida, Jacques. *Of Grammatology.* Translated by Gayatri Chakravorty Spivak. Baltimore: John Hopkins University Press, 1974.

Ducrot, Oswald, and Tzvetan Todorov. *Dictionnaire encyclopédique des sciences du langage.* Paris: Editions du Seuil, 1972.

Eco, Umberto. *The Role of the Reader.* Bloomington: Indiana University Press, 1979.

───. *A Theory of Semiotics.* Bloomington: Indiana University Press, 1975.

Fish, Stanley. *Is There a Text in This Class?* Cambridge: Harvard University Press, 1980.

Frye, Northrop. *Anatomy of Criticism: Four Essays.* Princeton: Princeton University Press, 1957.

Gadamer, Hans-Georg. *Philosophical Hermeneutics.* Translated by David E. Linge. Berkeley: University of California Press, 1976.

Genette, Gérard. "Genres, 'types,' modes." *Poétique* 32 (November 1977): 389-421.

───. *Narrative Discourse: An Essay in Method.* Translated by Jane E. Lewin. Ithaca: Cornell University Press, 1980.

Hellman, John. *Fables of Fact: The New Journalism as New Fiction.* Urbana: University of Illinois Press, 1981.

Hutcheon, Linda. *Narcissistic Narrative: The Metafictional Paradox.* Waterloo, Ontario: Wilfrid Laurier University Press, 1980.

Iser, Wolfgang. *The Act of Reading: A Theory of Aesthetic Response.* Baltimore: Johns Hopkins University Press, 1980.

Jauss, Hans Robert. "Literary History as a Challenge to Literary Theory." *New Literary History* 2 (Autumn 1970): 8-37.

Kayser, Wolfgang. *Interpretación y análisis de la obra literaria.* Madrid: Gredos, 1961.

───. "Origen y crisis de la novela moderna." *Cultura Universitaria* 47 (1955): 5-47.

Kellman, Steven G. *The Self-Begetting Novel.* New York: Columbia University Press, 1980.

Kristeva, Julia. *Desire in Language: A Semiotic Approach to Literature and Art.* Translated by Thomas Gora et al. New York: Columbia University Press, 1980.

Lanser, Susan Sniader. *The Narrative Act: Point of View in Prose Fiction.* Princeton: Princeton University Press, 1981.

Mailloux, Steven. *Interpretative Conventions: The Reader in the Study of American Fiction*. Ithaca: Cornell University Press, 1982.

Martínez Bonati, Félix. *La estructura de la obra literaria: Una investigación de filosofía del lenguaje y estética*. Barcelona: Seix Barral, 1972.

———. *Fictive Discourse and the Structures of Literature: A Phenomenological Approach*. Translated by Philip W. Silver. Ithaca: Cornell University Press, 1981.

Ong, Walter J., S.J. "The Writer's Audience Is Always a Fiction." *Publications of the Modern Language Association of America* 90 (January 1975): 9-21

Ortega y Gasset, José. *La deshumanización del arte*. Madrid: Revista de Occidente, 1925.

Pérez Firmat, Gustavo. "Apuntes para un modelo de la intertextualidad en literatura." *Romanic Review* 69 (1978): 1-14.

———. "Metafiction Again." *Taller Literario* 1 (Fall 1980): 30-38.

Pratt, Mary Louise. *Toward a Speech Act Theory of Literary Discourse*. Bloomington: Indiana University Press, 1977.

Rimmon-Kenan, Shlomith. "Ambiguity and Narrative Levels: Christine Brooke-Rose's *Thru*." *Poetics Today* 3 (1982): 21-32.

Scholes, Robert. *Fabulation and Metafiction*. Urbana: University of Illinois Press, 1979.

———. "Metafiction." *Iowa Review* 1 (1970): 100-115.

———. *Structuralism in Literature: An Introduction*. New Haven: Yale University Press, 1974.

Stanzel, Franz. *Narrative Situations in the Novel: Tom Jones, Moby-Dick, The Ambassadors, Ulysses*. Translated by James P. Pusack. Bloomington: Indiana University Press, 1971.

Stark, John O. *The Literature of Exhaustion*. Durham: Duke University Press, 1974.

Suleiman, Susan, and Inge Crosman, eds. *The Reader in the Text: Essays on Audience and Interpretation*. Princeton: Princeton University Press, 1980.

Todorov, Tzvetan. *The Fantastic: A Structural Approach to a Literary Genre*. Translated by Richard Howard. Ithaca: Cornell University Press, 1975.

———. "The Origin of Genres." *New Literary History* 13 (Autumn 1967): 159-70.

———. *The Poetics of Prose*. Translated by Richard Howard. Ithaca: Cornell University Press, 1977.

Tompkins, Jane P., ed. *Reader-Response Criticism: From Formalism to Post-Structuralism*. Baltimore: Johns Hopkins University Press, 1980.

Verdín Díaz, Guillermo. *Introducción al estilo indirecto libre en español*. Madrid: C.S.I.C., 1970.

White, Hayden. *Metahistory: The Historical Imagination in Nineteenth-Century Europe.* Baltimore: Johns Hopkins University Press, 1973.

Wicks, Ulrich. "The Nature of Picaresque Narrative: A Modal Approach." *Publications of the Modern Language Association of America* 89 (March 1974): 240-49.

Criticism

Bernstein, J.S. *Benjamín Jarnés.* New York: Twayne, 1972.

Bieder, Maryellen. "De *Señas de identidad* a *Makbara:* Estrategia narrativa en las novelas de Juan Goytisolo." *Revista Iberoamericana* 116-17 (July-December 1981): 89-96.

Bixler, Jacqueline Eyring. "Self-Conscious Narrative and Metatheatre in *Un hombre que se parecía a Orestes.*" *Hispania* 67 (May 1984): 214-20.

Blanco Aguinaga, Carlos. "Unamuno's *Niebla:* Existence and the Game of Fiction." *Modern Language Notes* 79 (1964): 188-205.

Buckley, Ramón, and John Crispin. *Los vanguardistas españoles (1925-1935).* Madrid: Alianza, 1973.

Castro, Américo. *El pensamiento de Cervantes.* Barcelona: Noguer, 1972.

de Nora, Eugenio. *La novela española contemporánea.* Vol. 2. Madrid: Gredos, 1962.

Díaz, Janet W. "Origins, Aesthetics and the 'Nueva Novela Española.'" *Hispania* 59 (March 1976): 109-17.

Díaz Migoyo, Gonzalo. *Estructura de la novela: Anatomía de "El Buscón."* Madrid: Editorial Fundamentos, 1978.

El cosmos de "Antagonía": Incursiones en la obra de Luis Goytisolo. Prologue by Salvador Clotas. Barcelona: Editorial Anagrama, 1983.

Emilio González, José. "Reflexiones sobre *Niebla,* de Unamuno." *Asomante* 17 (1961): 60-69.

Entrambasaguas, Joaquín de. *Las mejores novelas contemporáneas.* Vol. 7. Barcelona: Planeta, 1961.

Foster, David William. *Unamuno and the Novel as Expressionistic Conceit.* Hato Rey, Puerto Rico: Inter American University Press, 1973.

Fuentes, Víctor. "La dimensión estético-erótica y la novelística de Jarnés." *Cuadernos Hispanoamericanos* 235 (July 1969): 26-37.

———. "La narrativa española de vanguardia (1923-1931): Un ensayo de interpretación." *Romanic Review* 63 (October 1972): 211-18.

Gazarian Gautier, Marie-Lise. "Conversación con Carmen Martín Gaite en Nueva York." *Insula* 411 (February 1981): 1, 10-11.

Gerhardt, Mia I. *Don Quijote: La vie et les livres.* Amsterdam: N.V. Noord-Hollandsche, 1955.

Goytisolo, Juan, and Julián Ríos. "Juan Goytisolo-Julián Ríos: Desde *Juan sin Tierra*." In *Juan sin Tierra*. Madrid: Espiral/Revista, 1977.

Grande, Félix. "Narrativa, realidad y España actuales: Historia de un amor difícil." *Cuadernos Hispanoamericanos* 101 (May 1975): 545-51.

Hernández, Miguel Angel. *Prosa vanguardista en la generación del 27 (Gecé y La Gaceta Literaria)*. Madrid: Prensa Española, 1975.

Herzberger, David K. "Luis Goytisolo's *Recuento:* Towards a Reconciliation of the Word/World Dialectic." *Anales de la Novela de Posguerra* 3 (1978): 39-55.

Ilie, Paul. "Benjamín Jarnés: Aspects of the Dehumanized Novel." *Publications of the Modern Language Association of America* 76 (1961): 247-53.

Jdidi Embarec, Malika. "Lectura marroquí de *Makbara*." *Voces* 1 (1981): 83-86.

Kronik, John W. "*El amigo Manso* and the Game of Fictive Autonomy." *Anales Galdosianos* 12 (1977): 71-94.

———. "Galdós and the Grotesque." *Anales Galdosianos*, Anejo (1976): 39-54.

———. "Galdosian Reflections: Feijoo and the Fabrication of Fortunata." *Modern Language Notes* 97 (1982): 1-40.

———. "*Misericordia* as Metafiction." *Homenaje a Antonio Sánchez Barbudo: Ensayos de literatura española moderna*, edited by Benito Brancaforte et al., pp. 37-50. Madison: University of Wisconsin Press, 1981.

Levine, Linda Gould. "*Makbara:* Entre la espada y la pared—¿política marxista o política sexual?" *Revista Iberoamericana* 116-17 (July-December 1981): 97-106.

Levine, Susan F. " 'Cuerpo' y 'no-cuerpo'—Una conjunción entre Juan Goytisolo y Octavio Paz." *Journal of Spanish Studies: Twentieth Century* 5 (Fall 1977): 123-35.

Livingstone, Leon. "The Novel as Self-Creation." In *Unamuno, Creator and Creation*, edited by José Rubia Barcia and M.A. Zeitlin, pp. 92-115. Berkeley: University of California Press, 1967.

———. *Tema y forma en las novelas de Azorín*. Madrid: Gredos, 1970.

Marinero, Pacho. "Don Alvaro de Bretaña: Perífrasis y paráfrasis del tiempo." *Insula* 308-9 (July-August 1972): 23.

Martínez Cachero, J.M. *La novela española entre 1939 y 1969*. Madrid: Editorial Castalia, 1973.

Martínez Latre, María Pilar. *La novela intelectual de Benjamín Jarnés*. Zaragoza: Institución Fernando el Católico, 1979.

Matamoro, Blas. "Carmen Martín Gaite: El viaje al cuarto de atrás." *Cuadernos Hispanoamericanos* 351 (September 1979): 581-605.

Molina, César Antonio. "Alvaro Cunqueiro: La fabulación sin fin." *Insula* 413 (April 1981): 1, 10-11.

Ortega, José. "Aspectos narrativos en *Los verdes de mayo hasta el mar*, de Luis Goytisolo." *Cuadernos Hispanoamericanos* 370 (April 1981): 105-14.

Ortega y Gasset, José. *Meditaciones del Quijote*. Madrid: Espasa-Calpe, 1964.

Palley, Julián. "El interlocutor soñado de *El cuarto de atrás*, de Carmen Martín Gaite." *Insula* 404-5 (July-August 1980): 22.

Parker, Alexander A. "On the Interpretation of *Niebla*." In *Unamuno, Creator and Creation*, edited by José Rubia Barcia and M.A. Zeitlin, pp. 116-38. Berkeley: University of California Press, 1967.

Pérez Firmat, Gustavo. *Idle Fictions: The Hispanic Vanguard Novel, 1926-1934*. Durham: Duke University Press, 1983.

———. "*Locura y muerte de nadie:* Two Novels by Jarnés." *Romanic Review* 72 (1981): 66-78.

———. "Pedro Salinas' 'Mundo cerrado' and Hispanic Vanguard Fiction." In *La Chispa '81: Selected Proceedings*, pp. 261-67. New Orleans: Tulane University, 1981.

Riccio, Alexandra. "De las ruinas al taller en la obra de Luis Goytisolo." *Anales de la Novela de Posguerra* 2 (1977): 31-42.

Rico, Francisco. *La novela picaresca y el punto de vista*. Barcelona: Seix Barral, 1969.

Ríos, Julián, ed. *Juan sin Tierra*. [A collection of essays on the novel.] Madrid: Espiral/Revista, 1977.

Servodidio, Mirella d'Ambrosio, and Marcia L. Welles, eds. *From Fiction to Metafiction: Essays in Honor of Carmen Martín-Gaite*. Lincoln: Society of Spanish and Spanish-American Studies, 1983.

Sobejano, Gonzalo. *Novela española de nuestro tiempo (En busca del pueblo perdido)*. Madrid: Editorial Prensa Española, 1970.

———. "Valores figurativos y compositivos de la soledad en la novela de Juan Goytisolo." *Revista Iberoamericana* 47 (July-December 1981): 81-88.

Soldevila Durante, Ignacio. *La novela desde 1936*. Madrid: Alhambra, 1980.

Spires, Robert C. "*La cólera de Aquiles:* Un texto producto del lector." *Revista Iberoamericana* 47 (1981): 241-45.

———. "From Neorealism and the New Novel to the Self-Referential Novel: Juan Goytisolo's *Juan sin Tierra*." *Anales de la Narrativa Española Contemporánea* 5 (1980): 73-82.

———. "Latrines, Whirlpools, and Voids: The Metafictional Mode of *Juan sin Tierra*." *Hispanic Review* 48 (Spring 1980): 151-69.

———. "Letrinas, torbellinos y vacíos: el modo metaficcional de *Juan sin Tierra*." *Voces* 1 (1982): 67-79.

———. *La novela española de posguerra: Creación artística y experiencia personal*. Madrid: CUPSA, 1978.

———. "El nuevo lenguaje de la nueva novela." *Insula* 396-97 (1979): 6-7.
Thomas, Michael D. "Cunqueiro's *Un hombre que se parecía a Orestes:* A Humorous Revitalization of an Ancient Myth." *Hispania* 61 (March 1978): 35-45.
Toro, Fernando de. "Personaje autónomo, lector y autor en Miguel de Unamuno." *Hispania* 64 (September 1981): 360-65.
Ugarte, Michael. *Trilogy of Treason: An Intertextual Study of Juan Goytisolo.* Columbia: University of Missouri Press, 1981.
Van Ghent, Dorothy. *The English Novel: Form and Function.* New York: Harper and Row, 1967.
Villanueva, Darío. "La novela española en 1978." *Anales de la Narrativa Española Contemporánea* 4 (1979): 91-115.
———, ed. *La novela lírica, II: Pérez de Ayala, Jarnés.* Madrid: Taurus Ediciones, 1983.
Weber, Frances W. "Unamuno's *Niebla:* From Novel to Dream." *Publications of the Modern Language Association of America* 88 (March 1973): 209-18.
Zuleta, Emilio de. *Arte y vida en la obra de Benjamín Jarnés.* Madrid: Gredos, 1977.

Editions of Novels and Stories Quoted

Cervantes Saavedra, Miguel. *El ingenioso Hidalgo don Quijote de la Mancha.* 8 vols. Madrid: Espasa-Calpe, 1958.
[*The Ingenious Gentleman Don Quijote de la Mancha.* Translated by Samuel Putman. New York: Random House, 1949.]
Cunqueiro, Alvaro. *Un hombre que se parecía a Orestes.* Barcelona: Destino, 1969.
Goytisolo, Juan. *Juan sin Tierra.* Barcelona: Seix Barral, 1975.
[*Juan the Landless.* Translated by Helen R. Lane. New York: Viking Press, 1977.]
———. *Makbara.* Barcelona: Seix Barral, 1980.
Goytisolo, Luis. *La cólera de Aquiles.* Barcelona: Seix Barral, 1979.
———. *Recuento.* Barcelona: Seix Barral, 1973.
———. *Teoría del conocimiento.* Barcelona: Seix Barral, 1981.
———. *Los verdes de mayo hasta el mar.* Barcelona: Seix Barral, 1976.
Jarnés, Benjamín. *Locura y muerte de nadie.* Vol. 7 of *Las mejores novelas contemporáneas*, edited by Joaquín de Entrambasaguas. Barcelona: Planeta, 1961.
———. *La novia del viento.* Mexico City: Nueva Cultura, 1940.
———. *Teoría del zumbel.* Madrid: Espasa-Calpe, 1930.

Martín Gaite, Carmen. *El cuarto de atrás*. Barcelona: Destino, 1978.
[*The Back Room*. Translated by Helen R. Lane. New York: Columbia University Press, 1983.]
Pérez Galdós, Benito. *La de Bringas*. *Obras Completas*, 4: 1573-1671. Madrid: Bolaños y Aguilar, 1960.
  [*The Spendthrifts*. Translated by Gamel Woolsey. New York: Farrar, Straus and Young, 1952.]
———. "La novela en el travía." *Obras completas*, 6: 503-15. Madrid: Bolaños y Aguilar, 1945.
Quevedo, Francisco de. *Historia de la vida del Buscón*. Madrid: Espasa-Calpe, 1967.
[*The Swindler*. In *Two Spanish Picaresque Novels*. Translated by Michael Alpert. New York: Penguin, 1969.]
Tomeo, Javier. *El castillo de la carta cifrada*. Barcelona: Editorial Anagrama, 1979.
Torrente Ballester, Gonzalo. *Don Juan*. Barcelona: Destino, 1963.
———. *Fragmentos de Apocalipsis*. Barcelona: Destino, 1977.
Unamuno, Miguel de. *Niebla*. Madrid: Espasa-Calpe, 1963.
[*Mist*. Translated by Warner Fite. New York: Knopf, 1928.]
———. *San Manuel Bueno, mártir*. New York: Las Americas Publishing Co., 1960.

Index

act of discourse: as relates to Spanish self-referential novel, x, 73. *See also* discourse-focused novels
act of reading: as relates to Spanish self-referential novel, x, 73. *See also* reader-focused novels
act of writing: as relates to Spanish self-referential novel, x, 73, 107. *See also* author-focused novels
Aeschylus, 62, 67, 71
Alter, Robert, 1-2, 18, 25, 57, 133n. 8, 136n. 3
amigo Manso, El [Good Friend Manso] (Pérez Galdós), 26
Antagonía [Antagonism] (L. Goytisolo), 74, 109
anti-novel: as label for metafiction, 125
art for art's sake: and vanguardist literature, 45, 47, 58
artistic unity: rebelling against in *Un hombre que se parecía a Orestes*, 70
author-focused novels: defined, x, 73, 106-7; as represented by *Recuento*, 73-74; by *Los verdes de mayo hasta el mar*, 74-76; by *Novela de Andrés Choz*, 76; by *Juan sin Tierra*, 76-88
autotextualité, 33
Azorín, 33, 67, 71

Bal, Mieke, 138n. 10
Barthes, Roland, 114, 126
Beckett, Samuel, 2
Benveniste, Emile, 14
binary oppositions: as analyzed in *Juan sin Tierra*, 78-88
Bixler, Jacqueline Eyring, 136n. 11
Booth, Wayne, 12, 99
Bringas, La de [The Spendthrifts] (Pérez Galdós), 26

Brushwood, John S., 130n. 16
Buscón, El [The Swindler] (Quevedo), x, 11, 18, 23-25, 31

camino, El [The Road] (Delibes), 58
castillo de la carta cifrada, El [The Castle of the Coded Letter] (Torneo), 93-94
Castro, Américo, 18, 131n. 2
Cela, Camilo José, 4, 58
Cervantes, Miguel de Saavedra, 18-23, 27, 31, 32, 44, 46, 88, 126
Chatman, Seymour, 130nn. 19, 22
Christensen, Inger, 2, 3
Cinco horas con Mario [Five Hours with Mario] (Delibes), 89, 94
codes, 45-50; transformation of cultural into narrative in *Juan sin Tierra*, 78-88
cólera de Aquiles, La [Achilles' Rage] (L. Goytisolo), x, 89, 94-106
colmena, La [The Hive] (Cela), 58
comedy, 6-10. *See also* mode
Cooperative Principle, 125
Crosman, Inge, 138n. 12
cuarto de atrás, El [The Back Room] (Martín Gaite), x, 107, 113-24
Cunqueiro, Alvaro, 61-71, 88
curandero de su honra, El [The Healing of His Honor] (Pérez de Ayala), 33

dehumanization, 46
Delibes, Miguel, 58, 89, 94
de Nora, Eugenio, 134n. 2
Derrida, Jacques, 104
Díaz Migoyo, Gonzalo, 132n. 10
Dickens, Charles, 6
discourse-focused novels: defined, 73, 106-7; as represented by *Makbara*, 108-9; by *Teoría del conocimiento*,

109-13; by *El cuarto de atrás*, 113-24.
See also act of discourse
Doña Inés (Azorín), 33; as model for *Un hombre que se parecía a Orestes*, 67-71
Don Juan (Torrente Ballester), x, 58, 59-61

editorial narrator. *See* intrusive narrator
Enchained Andromeda (Rubens), 52
Entrambasaguas, Joaquín de, 134n. 2
erasure, under, 104

Fabulation and Metafiction, 7
familia de Pascual Duarte, La [The Family of Pascual Duarte] (Cela), 4, 13, 58
fantastic, the, 9; role in *El cuarto de atrás*, 118-24. *See also* mode
Fielding, Henry, 27
Fiesta al noroeste [Northeast Festival] (Matute), 58
flouting: as relates to violations of fictional modes, 125
focalization: as analyzed in *El Buscón*, 24-25; in *Locura y muerte de nadie*, 48; in *La cólera de Aquiles*, 99
Fortunata y Jacinta (Pérez Galdós), 26
Fragmentos de Apocalipsis [Fragments of the Apocalypse] (Torrente Ballester), 90-93
framing devices: as analyzed in *Niebla*, 34-44; in *Un hombre que se parecía a Orestes*, 61-71
Franco, Francisco: death of, 128
Frye, Northrop, 5-7, 9-10
Fuentes, Víctor, 134n. 2

Gaceta Literaria, La, 50
Galdós. *See* Pérez Galdós
Generation of '98, x, 33-34, 45
Genette, Gérard, ix, 3, 5, 14-15, 130n. 21, 131n. 23
genre, 3-6, 10-11, 72-73, 128
Gerhardt, Mia I., 131n. 6
Gómez de la Serna, Ramón, 56
Goytisolo, Juan, 76-88, 107-9

Goytisolo, Luis, 74-76, 94-106, 109-13, 131n. 1
Great Expectations (Dickens), 6
grotesque, the, 9. *See also* mode

Heidegger, Martin, 104
Hellman, John, 130n. 16
historical narrative, 117
history, 6-10. *See also* mode
hombre que se parecía a Orestes, Un [A Man Who Resembled Orestes] (Cunqueiro), x, 58, 61-71
Hutcheon, Linda, 2, 3, 133n. 4

implied author, 12, 100, 102, 108
implied reader, 5, 12
instances de discours, 14. *See also* narrating
interior duplication: as novelistic self-commentary, 33
intertextuality: as analyzed in *Locura y muerte de nadie*, 45-50; in *Don Juan*, 59-61; in *Un hombre que se parecía a Orestes*, 61-71; in *El cuarto de atrás*, 113-24
intrusive narrator, 31; as analyzed in *Locura y muerte de nadie*, 47
irony, 5. *See also* mode
Iser, Wolfgang, 12

Jarama, El [One Day of the Week] (Sánchez Ferlosio), 58
Jarnés, Benjamín, x, 45-57, 59, 71, 88
Juan sin Tierra [Juan the Landless] (J. Goytisolo), x, 72, 76-88, 95, 106, 107

Kayser, Wolfgang, 2, 18, 131n. 2
Kellman, Steven G., 2
Kronik, John W., x, 26, 133n. 7

LaForet, Carmen, 58
language: opaque/transparent, 9, 59; self-referential, 59
Lanser, Susan Sniader, 130n. 19
Lazarillo de Tormes, 11, 25
Levine, Susan F., 137n. 8

Index

literary models: transformation of as novelistic self-commentary in *Don Juan* and *Un hombre que se parecía a Orestes*, 58-71
Literature of Exhaustion, The (Stark), 2
Livingston, Leon, 133n. 2
Locura y muerte de nadie [The Insanity and Death of Nobody] (Jarnés), x, 45-50, 52, 135n. 11

Makbara (J. Goytisolo), 108-9
Marsé, Juan, 4, 94
Martínez Bonati, Félix, ix, 96, 131n. 25
Martínez Latre, María Pilar, 134n. 2
Martín Gaite, Carmen, 113-24
Martín-Santos, Luis, 59
Matute, Ana María, 58
Meaning of Metafiction, The (Christensen), 2
Merino, José María, 76
metafiction: as defined by others, 1-3; diegetically self-aware, 2; discursive, 2; linguistically self-reflective, 2; narrative, 2. *See also* mode
mimetic: high, 5; low, 5. *See also* mode
mimetic/nonmimetic language: defined, 96; as analyzed in *La cólera de Aquiles*, 96-99
Misericordia [Piety] (Pérez Galdós), 26, 139n. 8
mode: metafictional, ix, 1-3, 5-7, 9-10, 14-17, 72-73, 125; defined as linguistic phenomenon, 1-11, 14-17, 128; compared to genre, 3-4, 11
movement, literary, 4, 10, 72-73, 128
muchacha de las bragas de oro, La [The Girl with the Golden Panties] (Marsé), 94
myth, 5-11. *See also* mode

Nada [Nothing] (LaForet), 58
narratee, 14-15. *See also* reader: text
narrating: act of, 14, 19, 130n. 21; instance, 71, 107; process/product in *Juan sin Tierra*, 76-88
narrating/experiencing self: as analyzed in *El Buscón*, 24-25; in "La novela en el tranvía," 29
Narrative Discourse, 14
narrative levels: defined, 14-15; violations of, 15-16; as analyzed in *Quijote*, 18-23; in *El Buscón*, 23-25; in "La novela en el tranvía," 27-31
neorealism, Spanish, 4, 58-59
New Novel, Spanish, 4, 59, 74
Niebla [Mist] (Unamuno), x, 33-44, 45, 126
non-novel: as label for metafiction, 125
Novela de Andrés Choz [Andrés Choz's Novel] (Merino), 76, 88
"novela en el tranvía, La," x, 18, 27-32
novelistic theory, 9-10. *See also* mode
novia del viento, La [The Wind's Bride] (Jarnés), x, 45, 46, 50-57

Oresteia (Aeschylus), 62
Ortega y Gasset, José, 18, 46, 131n. 2, 135n. 15

Pale Fire (Nabokov), 1
Partial Magic, 1
Pérez de Ayala, Ramón, 33
Pérez Firmat, Gustavo, 1, 2, 50, 132n. 17, 135n. 15, 136n. 4
Pérez Galdós, Benito, x, 18, 25-32, 44, 46, 72, 126
picaresque, 4-10; novel, 4. *See also* mode
Plato, 3-4
Poussin, Nicolás: as referred to in *La cólera de Aquiles*, 105
presuppositions: as analyzed in *El castillo de la carta cifrada*, 93-94. *See also* reader expectations

Quevedo, Francisco, 18, 23-25, 27, 31, 44, 46, 126
Quijote (El ingenioso hidalgo don Quijote de la Mancha) (Cervantes), x, 1, 3, 6, 18-23, 31, 72, 126, 128, 131n. 1

reader: real, 11-13, 89; text, 11-13, 89; text-act, 11-13, 16, 89 reader expectations, ix, 31, 126-27; as analyzed in *La novia del viento*, 50-57; in *Don Juan*, 59-61; in *El castillo de la carta cifrada*, 93-94

reader-focused novels: defined, 73, 88-89, 107; as represented by *Fragmentos de Apocalipsis*, 90-93; by *El castillo de la carta cifrada*, 93-94; by *La muchacha de las bragas de oro*, 94; by *La cólera de Aquiles*, 94-106. *See also* act of reading

readerly texts, 126

reader-produced novels. *See* reader-focused novels

Recuento [Recount] (L. Goytisolo), 74, 88

referents, transformation of: as relates to fictional modes, 7-10; as relates to realism, 30-31; as relates to metafiction, 88

reportorial fiction, 9-10, 72. *See also* mode

Revista de Occidente, 45

Rico, Francisco, 132n. 10

Ríos, Julián, 107

romance, 5-10. *See also* mode

Rubens, Peter Paul, 52

Salinas, Pedro, 56

Sánchez Ferlosio, Rafael, 58

San Manuel Bueno, mártir [Saint Manuel Good, Martyr] (Unamuno), 43-44, 133n. 6

satire, 6-10. *See also* mode

Scholes, Robert, 1, 5-11, 127, 129n. 8

second-person narration: as analyzed in *Juan sin Tierra*, 84-86

Self-Begetting Novel, The (Kellman), 2

self-conscious novel: as defined by Alter, 2, 57

self-referential novel, Spanish: defined, ix, 16-17, 62, 71-74, 107-8, 127-28; as represented by *Recuento*, 74; by *Los verdes de mayo hasta el mar*, 74-76; by *Juan sin Tierra*, 76-88; by *Fragmentos de Apocalipsis*, 90-93; by

El castillo de la carta cifrada, 93-94; by *La muchacha de las bragas de oro*, 94; by *La cólera de Aquiles*, 94-106; by *Makbara*, 108-9; by *Teoría del conocimiento*, 109-13; by *El cuarto de atrás*, 113-24

sentiment, 6-10. *See also* mode

sign of absence: as analyzed in *Niebla*, 37; in *La cólera de Aquiles*, 99, 104

sign system: as analyzed in *Niebla*, 34-44; in *Juan sin Tierra*, 76-88

situation d'énonciation, 14, 130n. 21. *See also* narrating

Spanish American War, 33

Spanish Civil War, 58

Spanish society: as reflected by self-referential novel, 127-28

speech act, 125; as relates to reader-response criticism, 11-13; as analyzed in *Fragmentos de Apocalipsis*, 90-93

Stanzel, Franz, 132n. 9

Stark, John O., 2

Stern, Isaac, 125-26

Stern, Laurence, 2, 27

story-focused novels. *See* discourse-focused novels

structure of differences: as analyzed in *La cólera de Aquiles*, 94-106

suspension of disbelief: as analyzed in *Un hombre que se parecía a Orestes*, 69; in *La cólera de Aquiles*, 103

Tale of Two Cities, A (Dickens), 6

Teoría del conocimiento [Theory of Knowledge] (L. Goytisolo), 109-13

text vs. work, 12-13, 114

Tiempo de silencio [Time of Silence] (Martín-Santos), 59

Tigre Juan [Tiger Juan] (Pérez de Ayala), 33

Tirano Banderas [The Tyrant Banderas] (Valle Inclán), 33

Todorov, Tzvetan, 9, 118, 121, 130n. 18, 131n. 26

Tomeo, Javier, 93-94

Torrente Ballester, Gonzalo, 59-61, 90-93
tragedy, 6-10. *See also* mode
Tristram Shandy (Stern), 3

Ultimas tardes con Teresa [Final Afternoons with Teresa] (Marsé), 4
Unamuno, Miguel de, 34-44, 46, 88, 126
Unnameable, The (Beckett), 2
unreliable narrator, 99

Valle Inclán, Ramón de, 33
Van Ghent, Dorothy, 18, 131n. 2
vanguardism, Spanish: as relates to Jarnés and literary codes, x, 45, 50, 59
verdes de mayo hasta el mar, Los [The Verdure of May All the Way to the Sea] (L. Goytisolo), 74-76, 88
violations of fictional modes: defined, 14-16, 125; of narrative levels in *Quijote*, 18-23; of narrative levels in "La novela en el tranvía," 27-32; of characters/author/reader in *Niebla*, 34-44; of literary codes in *Locura y muerte de nadie*, 46-50; of reader expectations in *La novia del viento*, 50-57; of literary models in *Don Juan*, 59-61; of literary models in *Un hombre que se parecía a Orestes*, 61-71; of narrating/narration in *Recuento*, 74; of narrating/narration in *Los verdes de mayo hasta el mar*, 74-76; of narrating/narration in *Juan sin Tierra*, 76-88; of author/reader in *Fragmentos de Apocalipsis*, 90-93; of author/reader in *El castillo de la carta cifrada*, 93-94; of author/reader in *La muchacha de las bragas de oro*, 94; of author/reader in *La cólera de Aquiles*, 94-106; of oral/written discourse in *Makbara*, 108-9; of oral/written discourse in *Teoría del conocimiento*, 109-13; of oral/written discourse in *El cuarto de atrás*, 113-24; pseudo-violations in *El Buscón*, 23-25

Western society: as reflected in the self-referential novel, 127
Wicks, Ulrich, 4
writerly texts, 126

Zola, Emil, 6
Zuleta, Emilia de, 134n. 2, 135n. 14

863.09 Sp4   360439
Spires, Robert C.
Beyond the metafictional
mode.

DATE DUE

Johnson Free Public Library
Hackensack, New Jersey